Acclaim for David

*World Peace, a Blind Wife, and Gecko Tails*

"Dr. Khorram has the wonderful gift of being able to make us think and laugh at the same time. I nearly always laugh out loud while reading his work. But, his stories never fail to make me stop and reflect on some global issue or one of life's big questions. He shares with us his unique and refreshing way of seeing the world."

Don Bader, MD
Global Health Consultant

"Dr. Khorram blends wit, wisdom, care and concern in splashing rainbow colors. His humor, like any good comedy, symbolizes greater depths of truth, pain and joy. Newcomers and old-timers to the islands will find his insights and observations filled with potential, caution and possibility."

Rev. Ewing W. Carroll, Jr., retired
United Methodist Pastor

"This man's writings define the meaning of peace in the Pacific. He takes us toward the calm harbors during the occasional typhoons and calamities in our daily lives."

Robert T. Torres, Attorney

"Dr. Khorram stimulates us to explore our own views."

Joseph Kevin Villagomez
CNMI Secretary of Health

"Dr. David Khorram brings to the literary field a lot of the virtues he brings to the medical field: Intelligence, excellence and insight laced with a heavy dose of humor, foresight and compassion."

Jeffrey C. Turbitt
Columnist, *Marianas Variety*

"A Renaissance man in the western Pacific is an image that has fluttered through my mind more than once while reading Dr. David Khorram's offerings. His astute thoughts, and knowledgeable commentary on wide-ranging topics, attest to his awareness and interest in life on many fronts. He has an ability to phrase things succinctly, humorously and creatively, and is not above trying to involve his readers in taking an active and positive role in the local and world community. He is a Commonwealth treasure."

Jeff Schorr
Field Representative
Office of Insular Affairs
US Department of the Interior
Saipan

"Dr. Khorram's writing is easy to read and insightful. His writings are humorous, philosophical, and always full of soul. Everyone can relate to the basic human experience that he shares. You will find yourself laughing out loud as you read some of his stories, and seriously re-thinking the human condition as you read his more philosophical writings. This is a must-read for anyone who enjoys the writings of a person who portrays an open mind, open heart, and a positive spirit!"

Senator Maria Frica T. Pangelinan
15th Northern Marianas Legislature

"Consider this the *Chicken Soup for the Soul of Micronesia*. Dr. David Khorram offers a potpourri of good advice, on-target observations and musings, all designed to make you healthier in mind and body, and, at the same time, the world a better and nicer place in which to live."

Bob Coldeen
Author of *Bumps in Paradise*

"David Khorram's stories of life in the tropics are like a chilled mango salad on a hot day: so refreshing you don't even realize they're good for you too."

Michael Ernest, Attorney

"David has a way of seeing the big picture while the rest of us are still trying to figure out how to open the box."

Angelo O. Villagomez
Executive Director
Mariana Islands Nature Alliance

"Find thoughtful intelligence here. And marvelous insights into daily life and lives. Oh, and add humor, balanced with compassion. David's thoughts are deep, profound, and he shares them with a lightness that compels you to keep reading... about life, and community and members of that community being like family and embracing the world... to make it better... for us all. You find yourself absorbed by his gentle challenges, then feeling compelled to meet them."

Annette Donner
Producer, *Guam's Liberation*

"Reading this book is like spending time with your favorite spiritual adviser, doctor, philosopher, humanitarian, mentor, and best friend. Dr. David Khorram wields his mighty pen to restore vision to his readers, helping us see ourselves and the world with sharper clarity. His sense of humor is, indeed, a bonus."

Cinta M. Kaipat, Screenwriter
*Lieweila: A Micronesian Story*

"David Khorram's mind is like a prism for our times. When wisdom shines through his mind, it manifests in beliefs that uplift us, ideas that inspire us, and challenges that urge us to live our lives on deeper, wider, more transcendent and colorful levels of understanding."

Walt F.J. Goodridge
Author of *Turn Your Passion Into Profit*

"Absolutely superb, eloquent to the max. I don't know how he does it, but David always has a way of cutting through the overgrowth, then holding up the thing that really matters and saying 'This is what we should be talking about.' And then he'll explain something so clearly that you find yourself responding with 'I knew it! I mean, I couldn't say it before, but now I can!'"

David Yamartino, Engineer

"Physicists accelerate atomic particles at tremendous speed toward each other in order to study the composition of the universe. Dr. Khorram has accelerated a car containing three wise men toward an on-coming car containing the Three Stooges. The result is a fascinating and often humorous consideration of our own humanity and our collective potential for greatness."

Lt Cmdr Randy Clark, retired
United States Coast Guard

# World Peace,
# a Blind Wife,
## and
# Gecko Tails

# World Peace, a Blind Wife,

## and

# Gecko Tails

Intriguing Thoughts from an Island on Making Life
Happier and Healthier, and Laughing Along the Way

## David Khorram, MD

Saipan, Mariana Islands

ISBN-13: 978-0-9800531-0-4
ISBN-10: 0-9800531-0-2

Published by Tiningo Press, PO Box 503900, Saipan, MP 96950 USA

Visit www.tiningo.com for additional information.

Printed in the United States of America
12 11 10 09 08 07      10 9 8 7 6 5 4 3 2

*Dedicated to Mara, my love,*

*and*

*to my sister, Jaleh*

# ACKNOWLEDGEMENTS

I would like to express my gratitude to those who have played an important role in the creation of this book.

To Jayvee Vallejera, the editor of the *Saipan Tribune*, and to its publisher, John Pangelinan, who have provided a forum for my writing. Thank you for giving me the latitude to write about anything that crossed my mind.

To Frances T. Demapan, for encouraging me to create this collection.

To Lynn Kuliekie and Edmund Perry, teachers, who many years ago gave me the confidence and desire to write.

To Carol Danelius, for her time and diligence in improving the manuscript.

To my friends Houdin Dehnad, James Oh and David Yamartino, for their ongoing encouragement.

To Sarah Johnson and Kirk Johnson. Their energetic enthusiasm for this project has been a source of sustenance.

To Anne Erhard, who has helped me persist when I wanted to quit. Thank you, Anne.

To Mark Robertson, my friend and colleague, whose skill and dedication as a physician have given me the peace of mind to give attention to writing. Thank you, Mark.

To my children, Nava, Arman, Jaleh and Kian, whose very existence encourages me to explore new ideas, and to live a little off-balance.

And, finally, to my beloved wife, Mara Blonigen Khorram, who has been a helpmate in all facets of this work. She encourages me when I need it most, and her presence is a shining light in my life. You are the Pacific's gift to me.

# CONTENTS

# FOREWORD

I often start my Monday mornings sitting in my office sipping my coffee, looking out over the bay and across the deep blue waters of the Pacific. I eagerly click my mouse, hoping my friend from across the waves has found the time to write another column. I am always amazed that he somehow finds the time in a schedule filled with chasing after four young kids, running an eye clinic, opening a new school, playing soccer and all the other incredible things this guy fills his week with. Where does he find the time? But thank God he does. His email arrives and my week is now transformed. I immediately forward it to my sociology students at the University of Guam. I ask them to read it and to come prepared to discuss it in class. The issues are so local, yet so universal. The ideas cut to the core of our collective mindset, and make us laugh, cry and sigh. We often carry them into our conversations and our lives.

I first met Dr. David Khorram when my wife and I moved to Guam a decade ago. I was fresh out of graduate school and full of excitement and wonder. Earning my doctorate in sociology from McGill University in frigid Montreal, Guam appeared to be the farthest point on the globe. Deep in my soul I wanted to live a life that counted; to make a difference in whatever way I could. And so my life began on these beautiful islands teaching at a university filled with students who shared my excitement. David moved to the Pacific some years before I did. He lived and worked in Samoa where he met his wife, Mara. They moved to Saipan in the 1990's and opened an eye clinic by the beach. Soon David was well known among the people, and he found time to travel in the region for work and service. I met him while on one of his visits to our island and we immediately became fast friends.

Since that first day I met David, I have grown to respect and admire him greatly. Through his humor and insight, people's minds and spirits are transformed. The columns that he has selected for inclusion in this book are as diverse as the coral reefs that surround us. Flipping through them I am drawn again to the story of how David brought sight to a man who had battled cataracts for years. As David completes the surgery and moves the operating microscope, the man screams, "I can see, I can see." Being an eye surgeon, David tells us that he sometimes forgets how meaningful his job is: "It's nice to feel the sweetness of someone else's joy once in a while – to become aware of the miracles that take place every day around us, sometimes close, sometimes far. And to remember the things that we take for granted, like sight, can be so dearly missed by others and so deeply cherished."

It is thoughts and stories like this that David shares through his column that find common ground among all. He reminds us that our most valuable resource – the one that will ensure our survival as we venture into the increasingly rough waters of the future – is our own people. He reminds us of the *Book of Proverbs,* "Where there is no vision, the people perish." He proposes that we envision a future for our community and our children where creativity, service, character and global understanding become the foundation upon which we build our homes, our schools and our economic, political and personal relationships. He opens our minds to the possibility that "true prosperity means awakening the possibilities of the spiritual and material well-being of all our islands' inhabitants, without distinction..."

His words often act as a loving guide helping us to understand some profound life lesson. But he will readily admit that it is often the goofy and humorous thoughts that sometimes get the most enthusiastic response. I am reminded of his account of a phone conversation with a woman who did not speak English very well. He called to invite a friend to dinner and the woman answered the phone. David captures the humor and the frustration of diverse people coming in touch with one another. The multilingual misunderstandings that the phone call sets in motion lead ultimately to the blind wife in the book's title.

This book does wonders to lift the soul rather than burden it. It helps the reader focus on the good, the positive in everything. The analogy of the mirror helps us understand the value of this approach. The human soul is likened to a mirror – if it is turned to the sun it will reflect the light and heat of that sun. But if it is turned toward the dirt, the squabbles, the decadency and dark side of human reality, it will reflect that same darkness. This book is refreshing because its ideas lift us up and allows us, even in times of great distress and hardship, to focus on the light that shines upon the dirt.

During one of David's recent visits to Guam, I was thrilled to hear that he had decided to publish this book. I told him that I could now finally use something even more thought provoking and relevant in my Introduction to Sociology class. I teach two large sections of this class each semester, and in recent years I decided that I wanted to give the students an opportunity to read and reflect on something meaningful and not necessarily a sociology text. After much consideration I chose *Tuesdays with Morrie*, a life-changing book my students love. Yet now I will replace it with *World Peace, a Blind Wife and Gecko Tails*. I am convinced it will offer my students an even greater opportunity to reflect on their own lives, their communities, and the world their children will inherit.

Kirk Johnson, Ph.D.
Mangilao, Guam
August 2007

# INTRODUCTION

The phone rang. It was Jayvee Vallejera, the editor of the *Saipan Tribune*. "I've talked it over with the publisher, and we like your ideas, David. But we want you to be a little more controversial."

"No way, Jayvee." I proposed to write this weekly column because I wanted to make the world a better place. Pick up a newspaper on any given day and you find catastrophe, tragedy, corruption, crime and other anxiety provoking news. I wanted to share news or knowledge that might make someone happier or healthier. I wanted to share ideas that might touch a heart, a mind, a soul. I wanted to tell some stories that might make someone laugh, just to laugh. Or maybe help someone change in some small way. "There's already enough controversy in the paper, Jayvee. This is something different. Work with me on this."

I think Jayvee was reluctant, but he agreed, and the weekly column, *Better Living* was born in November 2004. This book is a collection of the favorite columns from those first few years.

I live on an island in the South Pacific – a place of romantic idealizations. An island is a paradise, but it is also a highly compressed universe. Everything is close together. The depth of the island's beauty is obvious as you gaze into her eyes, but so too is the piece of spinach stuck between her teeth. They are both unavoidable. How you respond to the spinach is what defines your experience. And this holds true not just on an island, but anywhere.

Many of these columns deal with the issues that arise in this compressed universe. I strive to lend a new perspective to them. My intent has been to open minds to new ideas and possibilities. For this reason I rarely mention the specific issues at hand. By not getting lost in the details of the issues, I hope that the readers would focus on the underlying principles, in a calmer, deeper way. Some of the columns deal with health, medicine, and well-being. Others are simply stories to entertain.

The columns that I've chosen for this book are the ones that people enjoyed the most – the ones that people would stop me in the grocery store to say, "I loved your column this week." Rather than try to organize them by topic, I've left them in the order they were written. I haven't attempted to provide any context or explanation, trusting that the ideas are universal, and that you can get a sense of what must have been going on in the community to merit the ink.

As I approached the end of the first year of writing these columns, the Northern Mariana Islands Council for the Humanities came to believe that my writing was doing something to promote the humanities on our islands. In 2005 the Council took what must have been an unusual step, and awarded me – a doctor and a newspaper columnist – a Governor's Humanities Award, naming me "Outstanding Humanities Teacher." I was deeply honored. Nevertheless, it has not been lost on me that for all my profound commentary and erudite exposition, for all my delving into history, philosophy, ethics, culture, comparative religion, sociology, psychology, government, health and economics, the column that is re-read the most, and appears to have changed more lives than any other, is the one that explains how to make yogurt.

Once in a while, someone wonders what makes me write on such a broad range of topics. Well, I'm a doctor, so I suppose it's natural for me to write about health and medicine. I'm a Bahá'í, which leads me to spend some time each day consciously thinking about self-improvement, peace, civilization and the things that relate to the planet's spiritual and social organization. The themes are on my mind, and they leak out onto the page. The rest of the stuff – the silly stuff – is just evidence of the futility of keeping the inner goofball contained.

David Khorram
Saipan, Mariana Islands
August 2007

# 1

## AN EASY WAY TO HAPPINESS

Have you ever wondered how you can be happier? I recently came across a fascinating research project that studies gratitude and thanksgiving. Researchers at the University of California and the University of Miami are using scientific methods to figure out how we can be happier. In a nutshell, they have found that practicing gratitude has a positive effect on both physical and emotional health. You can easily incorporate some of their discoveries into your own day.

The Gratitude Project has conducted quite a bit of research over the past few years. Yet, of all their studies, one caught my attention because it showed that you don't have to be *naturally* grateful to feel happier. You just have to start *thinking* grateful thoughts to be happier. I realized, "Hey, I can do that! Anybody can do that!" In this particular study, the researchers took several hundred people who had the same measure of happiness at the beginning of the study. These people were randomly divided into three groups.

Over the next month they went about their lives as usual, experiencing what we all experience – good things and bad things, happy things and sad things, pleasant things and irritating things. There was only one difference among the three groups: they spent a few minutes of each day thinking about and recording three different things. One group was "neutral," just recording the events of the day; one group thought about the unpleasant experiences of the day – the "hassles"; and one group was "grateful" – listing the things for which they were thankful each day. At the end of the month, the researchers measured the level of happiness of the people in the groups.

Here is what the study found. The people who practiced gratitude were happier and felt better than the other groups. They experienced higher levels of positive emotions, life satisfaction, vitality and optimism and lower levels of depression and stress than the other groups. The people who were assigned to think grateful thoughts exercised more regularly, reported fewer physical symptoms, felt better about their lives as a whole, and were more optimistic about the upcoming week compared to those who recorded hassles or neutral life events. Participants who kept gratitude lists were more likely to make progress toward important personal goals.

Other studies by the Gratitude Project have shown that people with a strong disposition toward gratitude have the capacity to be empathic and to take the perspective of others. They are rated as more generous and more helpful by the people around them. Grateful people are more likely to acknowledge a belief in the interconnectedness of all life and a commitment and responsibility to others. They place less importance on material goods; they are less likely to judge their own and others' success in terms of their possessions; they are less envious of wealthy persons; and are more likely to share their possessions with others.

Does this all sound like something you would want? It sure does to me. More life satisfaction, vitality, optimism, less stress, the ability to make progress toward personal goals, a sense of interconnectedness, and generosity – wow, wouldn't that all be nifty! But what can we do to develop this habit of gratefulness?

Here are a few suggestions to help you incorporate gratitude exercises into your daily life. I started these practices about a month ago, and I've found that they really work. They take very little time and I feel about the happiest I've ever felt. Nothing has really changed in my life. That is, all my challenges are still there, and my life is more complex than ever. I'm just more focused on being grateful. And I do feel more energetic, at peace, and connected with those around me. I feel happier.

In the Gratitude Project, people created a written list each day. Setting aside a few moments during the day to write in a journal or to make a list is certainly one option. Another option that works well for me is to take a few minutes to simply think about the things for which I'm grateful. During my morning walk I spend the first five or ten minutes just naming the people and things for which I'm grateful. I say them out loud because it seems that if I don't, my mind wanders and I get distracted.

If you can't think of things to be grateful for, start with yourself and then expand your thoughts to your family, friends, community and the world. For example, I might start by saying, "I'm grateful for my health." And then I widen the circle and express thanks for my wife and my daughter and my son, and then the people in my neighborhood. I think of the people with whom I work and I say their names and see each of their faces – "Thank you for Alex and Emilly and Flor and Joanne and Lin and Mark and Mel and

Mitos and Selmo and Thelma." I'll widen the circle again, saying, "I'm thankful for this beautiful community and all the helpfulness and caring and diversity here." "I'm grateful for the natural beauty that surrounds us." "I'm thankful to be alive during such an exciting time in history."

Another idea is to express gratitude for the little things that might go unnoticed. "I'm grateful for toothpaste." (Just imagine the world without it.) "I'm thankful for having this umbrella during the rain." "I'm grateful for the people that deliver our water." Focusing on the little things helps you create awareness and shows that you can be grateful even on a bad day.

By starting with yourself, and thinking about these widening circles and relationships that surround you, or by focusing on the little things, it's easy to come up with quite a few things for which you can be grateful.

If you're inclined toward prayer, you can express your gratitude as a prayer – "Thank you, God, for my friends and family. I am grateful for each of them."

This habit of gratefulness is a wonderful gift to give children. On our drive to school each day, our family plays "The Gratitude Game." We take turns expressing the things for which we're grateful. This week, my four-year-old son was grateful for the rain that fills the ocean so he can go swimming, and for the road that helps us get to school. My six-year-old daughter expressed her gratitude for her teacher, Mr. Michael, her principal, Ms. Trish, and for the moon.

Are you a teacher? Have your classroom keep "Gratitude Journals" as a way of nurturing this habit of the heart.

Directing your thoughts toward gratefulness really takes no extra time at all. If you don't have the time to write in a gratitude journal, you can do what I do: name the things for which you are grateful while you're walking, or driving, or getting ready in the morning, or working out. If you can connect these gratefulness exercises to an activity that you do each day, then you're more likely to express your gratitude regularly. You can start directing your thoughts toward gratitude right now. Just take a moment as you finish reading this page. Pause and think about a few things for which you're grateful.

# 2

## A Typhoon Called Diabetes

Our islands sit in the middle of the Pacific Ocean's typhoon alley. Each year, we watch as one or two or more typhoons approach us and build strength. We know that typhoons can be devastating. They can take lives and destroy the things that we value. So, we prepare for them.

We are alert to signs that they are forming many thousands of miles away. Through the use of satellite images and science, we all watch for them. Turn on the TV any day of the week, and you can find the channel with the satellite picture of the region. As the typhoon begins to form and gains strength, we plot its course, trying to anticipate how close it will come and how strong it will be. Why? So that we can protect ourselves. We may not understand how or why typhoons form. We may not know how their paths are predicted. But we do know that they can cause lots of damage. And we do know that knowledge and science can help us protect ourselves from disaster.

As the typhoon gets close, the skies outside may still be blue and the waters calm, but you will find us boarding up windows, securing things that could blow away, buying bottled water and canned food, and filling our cars with gas. We are getting ready, even though the sun may still be shining. We don't wait until the disaster strikes, because then it's too late to prepare. The damage will be harder to control. We rely on the satellite pictures, and the path mapped out by the scientists, to help us prepare so that we can best protect our lives and the things we value.

We are used to these typhoons. They come into our lives year after year, and we can mark time by their names – Omar, Paka, Ponsonga, Chaba. Yet, there is another typhoon that has hit our lives; one that kills more people and causes more damage to our lives than the wind and water typhoons. It is a typhoon that comes into thousands of families, often quietly, without island-wide excitement. It is a typhoon called diabetes. Each year its devastating forces blind, maim, cripple and kill thousands.

So much of the damage that is caused by diabetes can be prevented. But we need to begin to think about diabetes the same way we think about an approaching typhoon. We don't turn off our TV and say, "If I don't look at the pictures, then the typhoon won't come." Yet hundreds of people stop monitoring their diabetes, believing that if they don't think about it, the typhoon called diabetes will not do any damage. Other people know about the complications of diabetes, but don't take the steps needed to protect themselves. They often wait until the typhoon is blowing full force, and then try to board up the windows.

Our people are coming to understand more about this typhoon called diabetes. We know the devastation it brings – amputations, kidney failure, dialysis, heart attacks, strokes, blindness. We are beginning to learn to protect ourselves and our families. Just like a typhoon, diabetes and each of its complications has its own warning signs – its own kinds of satellite pictures and weather reports. It is up to us to use the information provided by our doctors to protect ourselves.

Just like a typhoon, diabetes can be devastating. And just like a typhoon, not all of the damage can be prevented. Every year I see many patients who go blind, or lose a foot, or go on dialysis – people who work hard at controlling this disease. Yet I see many more who needlessly suffer because of lack of knowledge and lack of preparation.

# 3

## TSUNAMIS AND THE MARIANA ISLANDS

How do we know if a tsunami is on the way to the Marianas? This is a question that has been on the minds of many since the devastation that struck our neighbors in the Indian Ocean, with no warning. The loss of life has been staggering, and the worldwide response has been a sign of the oneness of humankind. Yet many of us may wonder how things might be different here, if a tsunami were to come.

The Pacific Ocean, unlike the Indian Ocean, does have a tsunami warning system in place. The Pacific Tsunami Warning Center (PTWC) was established in 1949 in Hawaii to provide warning to countries and jurisdictions around the Pacific Ocean. Tsunamis are classified as either local, regional or Pacific-wide. They can be caused by a variety of disruptions to the ocean, such as landslides, volcanic eruptions, meteors, and of course earthquakes. The most destructive tsunamis are caused by earthquakes, and for this reason, the PTWC monitors earthquakes.

There are some 150 sensors throughout the Pacific that scan for underwater earthquakes. If there is an earthquake of magnitude 6.5 or greater anywhere in the Pacific, then a signal is sent to PTWC. An earthquake must be of magnitude 7.5 or greater to generate a tsunami, so the 6.5 threshold is a safe threshold. If the earthquake is between 6.5 and 7.5, PTWC sends out a "Tsunami Bulletin," which will basically say that an earthquake has occurred, but there is no risk of a tsunami.

If the earthquake is greater than magnitude 7.5 – large enough to generate a tsunami – PTWC takes the next step. It checks automatic tide sensors in the area of the earthquake to see if a tsunami might have been generated. This is not an easy task. If PTWC thinks that a tsunami has been generated, they issue a "Tsunami Watch or Warning" A tsunami in the open ocean is not visible from the air or by satellite. In fact, the height of a tsunami wave in the open ocean may be only a few feet. The passing wave of energy actually extends from the surface all the way to the ocean floor, and so in the deep water, the passing tsunami may only be a gentle swell, unnoticeable by a boat or a ship out at sea. When the wave approaches the coastline, the water "piles up" and becomes a catastrophic wall of water that can be stories high. If you get onto the PTWC website during the next Tsunami Watch or Warning, you may see that the height of the wave is two feet at a particular sensor. If this sensor is in the deep ocean, this two-foot wave could become a forty-foot wave at a coastline. Just because it's a small wave out at sea doesn't mean that it's a safe wave. So, interpretation of the data from tide monitors can be quite difficult.

In general, there is no method to determine if a tsunami has been generated except by actually detecting the arrival of characteristic waves at the network of tide sensors. It's kind of a "watch and see" approach. But because tsunami waves can travel so fast – up to 600 miles per hour – there is an urgency to get the warnings out quickly. This is why about 75% of the Tsunami Watch or Warning that are issued are cancelled. Although in many ways it's better to be quick to issue warnings, the effect is that when 75% of the warnings don't result in a tsunami, people get tired of false alarms and are reluctant to evacuate every time there is a warning.

So, here we are in the CNMI, and the PTWC sends out a Tsunami Watch or Warning. How do we get the warning, and what happens once the warning arrives? I spoke to Mr. Rudy Pua, the director at the Emergency Management Office (EMO), who kindly explained the process. EMO is part of the Aeronautical Fixed Telecommunication Network (AFTN) which is an international message system that is used primarily by air traffic control, aeronautical information services and meteorological services. This message system is monitored twenty-four hours a day by EMO staff. When a Tsunami Watch or Warning comes in through AFTN, EMO contacts the National Weather Service in Tiyan, Guam to confirm the occurrence of the earthquake, and to see if any further information is available regarding the generation of a tsunami wave.

At this point, the "Early Warning System" is activated, which means the public is alerted. The public alert takes place through a call from EMO to 1080 AM radio station, which announces the warning. The alert is then picked up by the other radio stations. The Department of Public Safety is also notified, and its personnel fan out to low-lying coastal areas with bullhorns to inform the population to move to higher ground. "Higher ground" means the areas of As Matuis, Capitol Hill, Navy Hill, the NMC area, and the main road along Papago. You don't have to go to the top of Mt. Tapochao.

During the twelve years that I've been here, I remember about three tsunami alerts. During the first one, I lived in an apartment right on Beach Road. The tsunami alert came during the middle of the night. My neighbors and I found out about it the next morning. The two other tsunami alerts came during the day, and many of us recall the confusion and chaos, and the traffic jam going up Capitol Hill. With the current system, if a tsunami of serious proportions were to hit us, many of us would die. If you sleep through the bullhorn, or if you're at a secluded beach, or if no one around you is listening to the radio, you'll never have a chance to evacuate. Or you'll be stuck in the traffic and chaos when the tsunami hits.

Where I grew up, in a rural valley in the Appalachian mountains of Kentucky, there was a risk of tornadoes. The town had a siren system. Every Saturday at noon, the siren would sound for one minute, just as a test. We all knew that if we heard the siren at any other time, it meant "Tornado! Go to your basement!" I asked Mr. Pua if such a system had been considered for Saipan – a network of sirens around the island that would mean "Tsunami! Move to higher ground!" Mr. Pua reported that such a system had been considered, and may have even existed here in the past. But such systems are expensive to maintain, and for this reason, it has not been revisited.

It is widely recognized that even with improved predictability of tsunami formation, the challenge is to get the word out. This is especially the case in places like Southeast Asia, where many coastal communities do not have access to modern communication systems or transportation routes to higher ground. There is very little time, and people have to be prepared to evacuate at a moment's notice. It is a formidable challenge.

All of this reminds me of when I was a medical student; one of my professors asked me why I studied so hard. My response was that I was afraid that if I didn't know enough, someday someone might die. "David," he said, "even if you do know enough, someday someone will die." Even with the best of tsunami warning systems, the finest local alert system, and the ideal evacuation plans, inevitably, people will die. Perhaps this is the most sobering aspect of such cataclysmic events: that we are forced to pause and see our own mortality against the indiscriminate and awesome forces of nature. And perhaps the biggest individual challenge then is not just to come up with a good plan to escape death, but rather to come up with a great plan to live a meaningful life.

# 4

# REALITY: MATERIAL OR SPIRITUAL?

Did you know that the horizon is always at eye level? If you sit down, the horizon appears to go down. If you stand up, the horizon seems to go up. If two people are next to one another, one sitting and one standing, they can argue all day long about where the horizon is located, and they won't reach any agreement. Why? Their perspectives are different.

In order for people to be united, even on the most basic level, they must share some perspective on the fundamental nature of reality. In the broadest sense, there are two views of the nature of reality: either reality is primarily material or primarily spiritual. The first perspective holds that reality is made up of the things that are concrete – those things that we can experience with our senses. The spiritual perspective, on the other hand, holds that this material world, the world perceived by our five senses, is not really "real." True reality is something beyond this material world. This world is only a transit lounge.

The basis for the spiritual nature of reality comes primarily from religion. Most religions speak of an existence beyond this material existence. But even those that do not, or those belief systems that consider themselves "spiritual" but not "religious," place importance on non-materialistic concepts such as love, compassion, kindness, forgiveness, sacrifice and cooperation. Our happiness, our sense of fulfillment, lies in nurturing our spiritual nature.

Materialistic ideologies are often focused on acquisition. The thinking goes that we need to have more stuff, and when we do, we'll be happy. Two predominant ideologies of the twentieth century – capitalism and socialism – both have their roots in this materialistic view of reality. Their expressions differ vastly, but fundamentally, they are both ideologies concerned with material issues. They do focus on a positive outcome, namely, providing for people's needs, but they view the needs of humanity as primarily material needs. They hold that happiness or a sense of well-being arises when our material needs are met or surpassed.

Of course, even those of us who have a spiritual understanding of the nature of reality also understand that we live in a material world. It is just that we seek to make decisions that pertain to this material existence not purely on a materialistic basis, but rather on a spiritual basis.

Ironically, many of us who think that our understanding of reality is spiritual, actually hold a rather materialistic view toward our spiritual side. We often treat our spiritual values or our religious beliefs as just one more item in our set of possessions – just another of the things we own, that we enjoy, and that we set aside at times, usually in order to pursue some form of acquisition. The challenge to those of us who hold a spiritual understanding of the nature of reality is to allow that understanding to permeate all of our actions and all of our decisions.

So, what does all of this have to do with living a better life? Well, for me it has been only recently that I have tried to give serious thought to the question of, "What is my own understanding of the nature of reality?" and, of course, the subsequent question, "Do I live my life in keeping with this understanding?" Do I believe that life is about giving and sharing, but at the same time live as if my goal is to acquire more goods? Is there a conflict between my beliefs and my actions? Such a fundamental conflict can be a major source of unhappiness, anxiety, crisis and general grumpiness. Spending a few minutes thinking about our own beliefs regarding the nature of reality can help us align our day-to-day actions with what we hope we believe.

What are your perceptions of reality? What are our perceptions of reality as a community? I believe that most of us would like to believe that our perception of reality is fundamentally spiritual. Do we show this in our moment-to-moment life, in our interactions with the people we encounter, in our family relationships, in our government positions, in our business dealings? The daily challenge is to align our activities in a material world with our spiritual aspirations.

# 5

# PROSPERITY:
# MORE THAN THE ECONOMY

For several years much of the world has been concerned with improving our economies. Traditionally, the idea of development and progress deals exclusively with improving our material condition. This perspective holds that "prosperity" is a condition of having the material resources to meet and surpass our physical needs.

With this perspective, poverty is a state of having inadequate food, shelter and transportation. Prosperity is viewed as having really good food, a really nice house, and a super-duper way to get around. Development today is mostly concerned with this material definition of prosperity: the transformation from poverty to prosperity – from bread and water to red-rice and fried chicken; from the tin house to the mansion on the hill; from the walking path to the Pathfinder.

I propose that we take a broader view of the concept of prosperity – that we expand our thinking of prosperity beyond just "having better stuff." Since most of us accept that the true nature of reality is not merely material, then our view of prosperity can go beyond strictly economic definitions. Let's recast the concept of prosperity to take into account a more comprehensive world-view: Prosperity is a condition of thriving, of flourishing, with regard to not only our material well-being, but also with regard to our human capacities, our spiritual nature.

The idea of prosperity, in its fullest sense, can be defined as *"an awakening of the possibilities of the spiritual and material well-being of all of the planet's inhabitants, without distinction."*[1]

What do you think about this perspective? How would our current approaches toward our economy and growth be changed if we held this fuller view toward the idea of prosperity – if we shift our attention a bit away from a material perspective of the nature of reality to a spiritual perspective of the nature of reality?

Traditionally, secular leaders have left concerns for the spiritual side of life to spiritual and religious leaders. However, ultimately, we are all concerned with all aspects of improving the human condition. It leads to a distortion of the true nature of our reality when we focus our attention purely on our material needs, and don't take into consideration the human spirit. Expanding our view of development and prosperity to include concerns of the soul, forces us to ask new questions and to seek new answers.

Psychiatrist, Dr. James Oh, has pointed out, "Money doesn't buy happiness... but is sure helps ease the pain." It does remain true that the pain and burden of physical suffering can be lifted with economic development. But economic development can only take us so far. So often it appears that we do actually believe that money *can* buy happiness and that economic development alone can bring us peace, happiness and fulfillment. Our public policies focus on the economy as a means to making us happy. Sometimes this material focus occurs at the expense of "awakening the possibilities of the spiritual and material well-being" of all our community's inhabitants. Wouldn't it be interesting to charge our government leaders not primarily with the task of improving the economy, but rather with the task of putting in place measures and policies that would help awaken the capacities in all of us, and to awaken the spiritual and material well-being that is latent in our community?

If true prosperity means awakening the possibilities of the spiritual and material well-being of all our islands' inhabitants, without distinction, then our attention moves beyond simply measuring economic growth. What might it look like for our public policy to be based on other measures such as the level of satisfaction, the level of happiness, the flourishing of the human capacities in *every* individual in our community, the fulfillment of human potential?

These questions are a bit more difficult to address and measure than purely economic ones, and perhaps it is too broad a charge. A starting point might be to simply begin to ask these questions as we consider the future of our communities and their well-being.

# 6

## TOUCH THE HEART OF AN ARTIST

This weekend, visit the Flame Tree Arts Festival, and buy a piece of art. It is a small way of thanking the artists for their contributions to civilization.

The work of an artist is the work of the Divine, for the artist is involved in creation. The artist turns the abstract to the concrete, translates something from the world of the heart and spirit and mind into the material world. They bring beauty. They move us, uplift us, and touch our hearts.

It has been said that all art is a gift from divine worlds. *"When the light shines through the mind of a musician, it manifests itself in beautiful harmonies. Again, shining through the mind of a poet, it is seen in fine poetry and poetic prose. When the light inspires the mind of a painter, he produces marvelous pictures."*[2]

Art surrounds us. Beauty and symmetry and harmony can be seen all around us, and the heart takes pleasure and enjoyment in them. Commenting on the attraction and prevalence of art, one author has written, *"A beautiful house, a well designed garden, a symmetrical line, a graceful action, a well written book, pleasing garments — in fact, all things that have in themselves grace or beauty are pleasing to the heart and spirit."*[3]

Art is often relegated to the periphery of our educational systems, and thus many of us come to believe that art belongs in the periphery of our lives. Yet the richest cultures are those in which artistic expression is nurtured at the grassroots, where everyone has a means for creative expression. It can be said that without art, there really is no culture. And without art, there is certainly no great civilization.

This weekend is our community's opportunity to celebrate our artists — those amongst us who are more actively focused on creating beauty and expressing spirit. It is also an opportunity for each of us to allow art and beauty and creative expression to move us. It may even be a chance for some of us to explore the idea of the artist within us — to be inspired to try something ourselves, to cultivate a latent talent or yearning.

The life of an artist can be difficult. The work is often arduous. Many hours are spent alone. The act of creation can be long and strenuous. Inspiration can dry up. And the bills can be difficult to pay.

So, as you visit the booths, and meet the artists, thank them! When the singers sing, applaud wildly! When the dancers dance, shout "Wooohooo!" When you see the artists, shower them with praise! Celebrate their efforts! Appreciate their work! Buy something and say, "Wow!" Encourage them! Touch their hearts! Bring them chocolates!

# 7

## THE INCONVENIENCE OF PEACE

Like many people, I would like to have peace, just as long as I don't have to work too hard to get it. You know what I mean, right? I don't want to have to change or to be inconvenienced by the quest for peace. But as the saying goes, you can't keep doing the same thing and expect to get different results. So, like anything else, if I don't have peace and I want it, I'm going to have to change the way I think about things and do things.

Years ago I came across a statement about peace that has stuck with me: *"The well-being of mankind, its peace and security are unattainable, unless and until its unity is firmly established."*[4] This statement struck me because it goes against conventional thinking. The general expectation is that first we need to establish peace, and then we'll have unity. For example, in international relations, we take the view that if we first build peace with that country then we'll eventually become unified, and consider ourselves as one. But the statement above challenges this conventional thinking. It says there is no way to have peace until we first establish unity with that nation. Establish unity first, and then peace, security, and well-being will naturally follow. Without unity, there is no way we'll have peace.

On the surface, this statement seems to address the concept of global peace, which for many of us is a distant and abstract idea. In more concrete terms, I have plenty of "lack of peace" in my own life. Maybe that's a place to start. So, I begin to consider that this same principle might apply not only to world peace, but also to the day-to-day peace that we all want in our lives. In my mind, I begin to replace the word "mankind" with smaller and more intimate relationships. The well-being of this *family*, its peace and security are unattainable, unless and until its unity is firmly established. The well-being of my *workplace*, its peace and security are unattainable, unless and until its unity is firmly established. The well-being of my *government agency*, its peace and security are unattainable, unless and until its unity is firmly established. The well-being of this friendship, of these ethnic groups and cultures, of my interaction with my employer or my employees – every relationship or organization – its peace and security are unattainable, unless and until its unity is firmly established.

As I think more about this, I begin to see that pretty much every problem in the world can be boiled down to disunity. Wherever there is a lack of a sense of oneness, there is a lack of peace and security. Wherever there is a lack of appreciation for the idea of unity – that we are a "unit," one, the same on a deep fundamental level: that our feelings, our pain, our laughter and joys are the same – wherever this idea of oneness and unity is lacking, there is no peace.

Here is an example. Two ethnic groups are at war – maybe subtle war, maybe outright war. The world tries to solve the conflict by trying to first address issues of peace and security, without touching on the concept of unity. "Let's see," says the world, "First, everyone has to put aside their weapons. Next, let's draw some borders. You people all stay on this side of the line, and you other people stay on that side of the line. And let's see if this works. Maybe after a while, you'll be able to get along better and not kill each other any more." This is pretty much the same approach many of us parents take when trying to negotiate peace among our warring children (which is maybe where this approach toward international peace negotiations comes from) – make them stop hitting each other, send the kids to their separate rooms, and hope that when they come out, they'll get along better.

In both scenarios, sooner or later, war is going to break out again. The peace is temporary. The security is ephemeral because it was not based on unity. It's not based on the concept that despite our differences, we two people are really fundamentally one. Without establishing this concept as the fundamental basis for peace, the peace will eventually erode. I think this concept can be applied to all our relationships. First establish (or re-establish) the unity between friends, employees and employers, spouses, co-workers, members of government, businesses – whatever relationship might exist – and peace, security and well-being will be a natural and lasting outcomes.

So, maybe I'm a bit more convinced now. But, this raises a whole new set of questions. If I need to shift my focus to first establishing unity, what am I going to have to do differently? What is needed for unity to exist, especially in my daily life? I suspect it's going to be a bit inconvenient.

# 8

# A First Essential for Peaceful Relationships

L ast time, I shared how I became convinced that working for peace is futile without first working toward
building unity. This line of thinking came to me from
a statement I had read years ago: *"The well-being of mankind,
its peace and security, are unattainable, unless and until its unity is
firmly established."* [5] The next question that arises, of course,
is what do I have to do to establish unity? If I need to shift
my focus to first establishing unity, what am I going to have
to do differently? What is needed for unity to exist?

In considering this question, rather than thinking about
unity on an international or global scale, I began to think
about unity on a personal level. There is a principle that has
been identified as one of the "first essentials" of unity. It is
quite a simple principle, quite profound, and for many of us,
also quite difficult.

In order to achieve unity, one of the first essentials is
that we resist the natural tendency to let our attention dwell
on the faults and failings of others rather than on our own.

This does seem quite simple, but not easy. As I thought about this, I came to realize that in my own relationships, any time that unity is lacking, or that I'm not getting along with someone, or that I'm just unhappy about the way things are going, it is usually because I am dwelling on the faults and failings of the other person. I've come to realize that it really is hard to have unity when we dwell on one another's faults and failings. And without unity, there is no peace and security in the relationship.

Dwelling on the faults and failings of others is the first step toward disunity. I'm convinced that *any* disunity between people can be traced to the fact that someone is dwelling on the faults and failings of someone else. Resisting this tendency is the foundation of unity among people and the foundation of the peace, security and well-being in any relationship. It is essential. A peaceful relationship cannot exist without it. Think about some difficult relationships in your life. I'll bet that a big part of what makes them difficult is that the folks involved are dwelling on the faults and failings of one other.

One thing that struck me is that this tendency to dwell on the faults and failings of others is a natural one. We are all naturally inclined toward dwelling on the faults and failings of others rather than on our own. And like any natural tendency, it can be difficult to resist. After all, everyone has faults. Your parents have faults. Your boss has faults. Your neighbors have faults. Your employees have faults. Your children have faults. Your co-workers, your spouse, your housekeeper, your friends, your in-laws, your brothers and sisters, your community leaders – they all have faults. Even people that you don't know have faults! The cashier, the waitress, the person driving in front of you – by golly, everybody has faults. You can hardly swing a dead cat without hitting someone's faults. Every time you come into contact with another person, you are likely to get whacked by one of their faults. The key is to resist the natural tendency to dwell on their faults.

Not only does dwelling on the faults of others rupture the unity that may exist, it also makes you just plain unhappy. It's fair to say that you will never be happy as long as you dwell on the faults of others. The lives of the unhappy people I know are consumed with dwelling on the faults of others. By doing so, they fracture the security, peace and unity of the relationship, and they are miserable. It's no wonder that it has been said that the most hateful characteristic is fault-finding.

Early on in most types of relationships we resist this natural tendency. But as time passes, our attention begins to dwell on the faults and failings of the other. In the early days of the marriage, it's all love and romance. Love is blind to faults and failings. Later, the couple begins to see one another's faults. Those couples who dwell on those faults and failings eventually become buried beneath them. The new employee is bright and enthusiastic, a godsend, the best thing that ever happened to the place. But as time passes, everyone becomes aware of each other's faults and the cheerful mood dissolves. Does any of this sound familiar?

Unity is needed for peace, security and a sense of wellbeing. A first essential to having unity in a relationship is to resist this natural tendency to let our attention dwell on the faults and failings of others. To resist implies that one needs to make active effort. But how can we resist this natural tendency? Next time we'll discuss some practical strategies to resist the natural tendency of letting our attention dwell on the faults and failings of others. Until then, when things get rough in your interactions with another person, or even when you just become slightly unhappy with someone, ask yourself, "Am I dwelling on their faults and failings?" This is a first step toward bringing about unity and peace.

# 9

## LOOK IN THE MIRROR

Amazing thing, this internet, isn't it? Here is a question I received this week from a reader in Iraq: "I understand that dwelling on the faults of others destroys my relationships with people, whether it's my family, friends, co-workers or neighbors. It destroys the unity between us, and without unity, I know that peace and security are not possible. I also realize that dwelling on the faults of others makes me unhappy. But what can I do, practically, to *not* dwell on the faults of others?"

Well, that's the essence of it, isn't it? What can I do in real life when I'm faced with the faults of others? Here's a suggestion: change the subject. When we dwell on something – anything – we are allowing our attention to focus on a particular pattern of thoughts. If we want to stop dwelling on something, we simply have to shift our attention to another subject. Everyone has faults, and we'll encounter them with nearly every interaction of the day. It's a natural tendency to dwell on them. It takes a decision on your part to shift your attention somewhere else. We have to mentally change the subject.

But what should the new subject be? Where should my attention shift? What should be the new focus for my thoughts?

One of the first places to shift our attention is to *our own faults*. After all, I really am responsible for only one life, and that's my own. I only have control over one person, and that's me. I ran across these few sentences that sum it all up.

> *"Each of us is immeasurably far from being perfect... and the task of perfecting our own life and character is one that requires all our attention, our will-power and energy. If we allow our attention and energy to be taken up in efforts to keep others right and remedy their faults, we are wasting precious time. We are like plowmen each of whom has his team to manage and his plow to direct, and in order to keep his furrow straight he must keep his eye on his goal and concentrate on his own task. If he looks to this side and that to see how Tom and Harry are getting on and to criticize their plowing, then his own furrow will assuredly become crooked."*[6]

It's quite tempting to set about correcting Tom and Harry's plowing. But ironically, in the long run, you're happier when you shift your focus and your attention away from the faults of others and toward your own. After all, we can each actually do something about our own faults. Along the same lines,

> *"Whenever you recognize the fault of another, think of yourself. What are my imperfections? — and try to remove them. Do this whenever you are annoyed or exacerbated by the words and deeds of others. Thus you will grow, become more perfect. You will overcome self, you will not even have time to think of the faults of others."*[7]

Now, I'll admit, I dread being "tried by the words and deeds of others." But these ideas give me a new perspective. If I can really work on shifting my attention away from the faults of others, and toward my own, if I can muster up the discipline to do this consistently, to fight against my natural tendency to dwell on the faults of others, then an encounter with the faults of others is an opportunity to improve myself and my character. The key is to shift my attention away from others toward self – to look in the mirror. In the process I become a better person. Their faults are my opportunity to improve.

Chances are that within fifteen minutes of finishing reading this, you're going to get smacked in the head with someone's faults. (If you're reading this in my office, it might be me.) Rub the bump on your head and immediately decide to shift your focus away from their faults toward your own. Don't get anywhere near "dwelling" on them. View the encounter with their faults as an opportunity to shift your attention to your own faults and to improve your own character. After a while, it becomes natural, but it will take a decision on your part, and then effort and discipline.

# 10

## BENEFITING FROM LIFE'S TESTS

If you're ever lucky enough to find a lump of gold, you'll probably be unlucky enough to throw it away. You see, a lump of gold in its natural state is usually so full of impurities that it doesn't look quite like the gold you're used to seeing. You wouldn't recognize it as gold. To purify the gold, you need to subject it to extreme heat – melt it – and the dross floats away. The fire removes the impurities and the gold shines.

I picked up a book this week entitled, *Fire and Gold – Benefiting from Life's Tests,* by Brian Kurzius. The title implies that the purification of gold by fire is like purification of our characters by tests, trials and tribulations. The book points out that tests are inevitable. Growth comes only by being subjected to and overcoming tests. Without tests, there is no growth. Bummer. I was hoping on just relaxing – soaking up some water and sunshine and, you know, just growing without having to exert any effort – kind of like a plant. I wasn't really counting on test after test after test.

Kurzius points out that *"the challenge of tests is to use them to grow rather than complaining about their appearance. For if we look upon our suffering as an opportunity to grow, we transform our negative experiences into positive ones and can develop capacities and strengths that we never knew existed.*"[8] Wow. Now wouldn't that be different – to stop complaining because of the tests that come my way? To think of suffering as an opportunity to grow? To transform my negative experiences into positive ones? I need to shift my perspective so that I see these tests as a positive force in my life. If I do, I might actually be able to benefit from them.

It has been poetically stated that, *"Men who suffer not, attain no perfection. The plant most pruned by the gardener is that one which, when the summer comes, will have the most beautiful blossoms and the most abundant fruit."*[9] This statement is especially meaningful to me, since I have aspirations of being a plant. *"The mind and spirit of man advance when he is tried by suffering. The more the ground is plowed the better the seed will grow, the better the harvest will be. Just as the plow furrows the earth deeply, purifying it of weeds and thistles, so suffering and tribulation free man from the petty affairs of this worldly life..."*[10]

Got thistles? How about weeds? Petty affairs? That plow that's digging those furrows across your heart can serve a purpose. Just by realizing that trials and tribulations can serve a purpose, we can accept them, maybe even welcome them, and benefit from them. Tests and difficulties come again and again and help turn our weaknesses into strengths. They are a part of the rhythm of life, the cycle of growth. If we don't see their purpose, life is devoid of dignity and grace, and is usually one big complaint.

The next time I'm feeling pruned or plowed, or stuck in the fire, I'll remember to look upon my suffering as a means of purification of my character, as an opportunity to grow.

# 11

# TRUTHFULNESS: THE FOUNDATION

I've been participating in a course for the past few weeks entitled, *Reflections on the Life of the Spirit.* It originated at the Ruhi Institute in Columbia and has grown to be used by communities around the world. It explores the life of the spirit – the essence of being human. The first part of the course focuses on issues related to character development, and this is where we are now.

The section that we just completed was on truthfulness. One of the statements that raised a lot of discussion in our group was *"Truthfulness is the foundation of all human virtues."*[11] It's a bold statement. It implies that in the same way that a building cannot be strong without a firm foundation, one's character cannot be sound without truthfulness. After all, the essence of our character is the combination of virtues we possess – virtues like kindness, humility, generosity, courage and enthusiasm. To say that "truthfulness is the foundation of all human virtues" implies that we cannot truly possess the other virtues without truthfulness – that they are subject to erosion or collapse without the foundation – truthfulness.

In our discussion we realized that we all take it for granted that we need to be truthful. No one really believes that lying is a good thing. But we seem to believe that lying is a necessary part of life. Most of the structures of our society are based upon the prevalence of this belief that lying is necessary, and sort of okay. Our entire judicial system is really trying to answer the question, "Is the defendant lying or being truthful?" Any request for identification presumes that if you were asked, "What's your name?" you would lie. Time-clocks presume that if simply asked, "What time did you arrive at work?" you won't tell the truth.

Distorting the truth is considered a gymnastic sport – we "bend" the truth, or "stretch" the truth, or "spin" the truth, all the while somehow convincing ourselves that we're not *really* lying. And it's all these teensy weensy lies that erode the sense of security and trust within a community. We somehow want to believe that having someone else clock in for us when we're running late is not simply just a lie.

Of course there is always some fairly good reason to distort the truth (lie). The need to stay out of trouble and to avoid embarrassment top the list of reasons. Thinking of truthfulness as the foundation of all the other virtues and as the foundation of our character gives us reason to be more conscious about eliminating those little "harmless" lies.

The first thing that I noticed about being dedicated to truthfulness is that I have to live differently. If I'm going to have to be truthful about this action, and I won't be able to use a lie to get out of trouble or avoid embarrassment, then I might have to do things differently.

The next statement in the section was even more motivating, probably because for some of us, fear is still the number one motivator. *"Without truthfulness, progress and success in all the worlds of God, are impossible for any soul."* Whoa. That's a pretty strong statement. No truthfulness, no progress. No truthfulness, no success. Not here, not hereafter. Impossible for any soul.

As we discussed these ideas in our group, I think that we each found new reason to embrace truthfulness as a way of life, recognizing that it is the foundational virtue upon which character is built and that without it, progress and success are impossible.

How might your day be different if you were conscious throughout the day that truthfulness is the foundation of all human virtues and that without it, any type of progress and success are impossible?

# 12

## DEVIANT BEHAVIORS

My friend, Dr. Kirk Johnson, teaches a course entitled, *Deviant Behaviors* at the University of Guam. I always enjoy talking to Kirk, because, as a sociologist, he does pretty much anything he wants that's related to people and society, and he gets to call it work. Lucky Kirk. I was expecting this course on deviant behaviors to be about people outside the norms of society, like serial killers, or juvenile delinquents. But Kirk told me that the course was based upon the premise that we all have some kind of deviant behaviors – something we do, that makes us feel a little bit crazy or interesting or wild. Sometimes we do these things alone (like dancing on the table at home), or sometimes we do them while interacting with others. These days, a simple act of kindness, like letting someone turn in front of you when you're driving, can be classified as a deviant behavior.

I realized that exhibiting deviant behaviors is fun. Here are a couple of mine. My four-year-old son, Arman, loves to annoy his six-year-old sister, Nava. Almost invariably, when we're driving, I'll hear Nava yelling from the back of the van – "Dad! Arman's copying me!" I used to say something like, "Arman, Nava doesn't seem to like it when you repeat everything that she says. It's annoying her (as if he didn't know). Please stop." But as of last week, I have a new response. When Nava says, "Dad! Arman's copying me," I just say, "Dad! Arman's copying me!" Even kids enjoy deviant behavior, especially in their parents.

Another deviant behavior that eventually brings a smile to everyone's face is rhyming. Sometimes when I'm having a conversation with my wife, Mara, I'll decide that whatever she says, my response will rhyme with hers. "Good morning, David. How are you?" "Fine, Honey. Have you seen the grass covered with dew?" This can go on for quite some time without the other person realizing that you're rhyming with them. At some point, you'll start laughing.

A friend recently shared this list of fun deviant behaviors with me.

At lunchtime, sit in your parked car with sunglasses on and point a hairdryer at passing cars. See if they slow down.

Page yourself over the intercom. Don't disguise your voice.

Every time someone asks you to do something, ask if they want fries with that.

Put your garbage can on your desk and label it "IN."

Put decaf in the coffee maker for three weeks. Once everyone has gotten over his or her caffeine addiction, switch to espresso.

Don't use any punctuation.

As often as possible, skip rather than walk.

Specify that your drive-thru order be "to go."

Sing along at the opera.

Put mosquito netting around your work area. Play a tape of jungle sounds all day.

Five days in advance, tell your friends you can't attend their after-work outing because you're not in the mood.

When the money comes out of the ATM, scream, "I won! I won! This is the third time this week!"

Try one of these deviant behaviors and add a smile to your day.

# 13

## MEDICALLY UNDERSERVED

I've always said that our healthcare system in the CNMI is among the best in the region, and that the overall quality of physicians here is as high as in other rural communities anywhere in the United States. Yet our population is medically underserved. The resources for care, though good, are limited. There are not enough doctors to serve our population. The public health care facilities are often short of supplies and specialists. On the operating room wall hangs a quotation from Dr. Howard Tait, who served as the CNMI's orthopedic surgeon for many years. Speaking to other surgeons, he said, "If you have to have everything you need to do the case, you probably shouldn't be here." Strangely, these are the very reasons that many of us choose to practice medicine here. We get personal satisfaction from making a difference to the people we serve, and we love the challenges of not having everything we need.

The US Department of Health and Human Services routinely evaluates the access to care in all US jurisdictions and gives each geographic area a Health Professional Shortage

Area (HPSA) score. This HPSA score is an indication of how badly doctors are needed in an area. The scoring system used by the Department of Health and Human Services takes into account such factors as the number of doctors available for the population, and the travel times to the nearest available source of care. The higher the score, the worse off is the region, and and the more badly doctors are needed. A HPSA score of 25 is bad, 1 is great.

How do you think the CNMI ranks on this list? Well, it's pretty bad – in fact, among the worst. For non-metropolitan areas in Region IX, the highest shortage award goes to our neighbors, the Federated States of Micronesia, with a HPSA score of 25. There is no other area in the entire US with a greater need for doctors. This is followed by a few Native American Reservations in Arizona, California and Nevada that have HPSA scores between 21 and 19. Next comes American Samoa with a HPSA score of 20. And then, the CNMI with a HPSA score of 18. A HPSA score of 18 is bad. It is an indication that despite having one of the best hospitals in the region and having great doctors on the island, we are among the most underserved areas in the entire country. Guam fares much better than we do, with a score of 8. Many Native American Reservations have better HPSA scores and less of a doctor shortage than we have.

Areas that have doctor shortages typically do everything possible to bring in more doctors. There are tremendous challenges in bringing in new doctors to the CNMI. After all, the area is underserved for a reason. If it were considered a great place to practice medicine, there wouldn't be a shortage in the first place. This is one of the reasons that our public facility is constantly short of doctors and specialists. There has to be a compelling reason for people to move half-way across the world, to an unknown land, far from their families, and take a pay cut to work under challenging circumstances.

In my case, I had always wanted to work in an under-served area – to feel like I was making a real difference to the people I served. When I arrived in the CNMI in 1993 as a government employee, I thoroughly enjoyed establishing the first eye care services at the Commonwealth Health Center (CHC). It was a challenge, and I was able to make a big difference quickly. I saved the government hundreds of thousands of dollars in referral costs, and I had the privilege of making life better for my patients. After five years at CHC, my wife and I decided to make the CNMI home and realized that this would be difficult to do while working for the government. Each year there were questions of whether or not funding would be available for my position and whether or not my contract could be renewed. I had also reached the limit of what I could build under the government system. I came from one of the best centers in the US, and I wanted to bring in the best eye care technologies to the CNMI. The emphasis of CHC was rightfully on providing primary care to as many people as possible with the limited resources available, so it just wasn't feasible to spend money on the more advanced technologies I was requesting. For these reasons, and with the enthusiastic support and encouragement of the administration I entered the private sector. This is where I believe the future of improving health care in the CNMI lies. We will always need a government supported hospital. But one of the keys to addressing our poor HPSA score, and building a stable medical community is to encourage the development of private medical practices.

Most of us in private practice came to the CNMI as government employees. Dr. Tony Stearns' venture into private medicine resulted in the establishment of FHP (now

PacifiCare), and more recently of Marianas Medical Center. Dr. Hocog and Dr. Aldan built Saipan Health Clinic. Dr. Ahmad Al-Alou established Pacific Medical Center. Tony Glad built Island Medical Center. And most recently, Dr. Norma Ada has opened Medical Associates of the Pacific. Together, these practices, along with my own, remove the burden of some 60,000-76,000 office visits from the shoulders of the government facility each year.

Private practices provide stability and continuity of care. The average number of years that each of the physicians in private practice has served in the CNMI is somewhere between ten to fifteen years. We put down roots. Those of us in specialty care like me, provide support to other physicians, like those in the emergency room, when complex cases arise. Private medical offices are more likely to invest in the most advanced technologies which raise the level of care for the whole population. It was Dr. Al-Alou at PMC who had the vision and the means to bring the first CT scanner into the CNMI. Marianas Eye Institute brought in technologies that most eye care practices in the US mainland don't even have. Private medicine raises the level of care.

I list these benefits because I believe that stimulating the development of private medical practices can be more actively pursued in the CNMI. In Guam, we see that the entire medical care system, like that in every other developed jurisdiction in the United States, is built upon a strong and healthy private practice model. We need to actively attract doctors into private practice.

As a community and a government, we may wish to consider the big picture of healthcare, and of our severe physician shortage, and consider which legislation, policies and regulations – which decisions – will move us closer to addressing our doctor shortage, and which will take us further away. Quality healthcare for the greatest number of people is a guiding principle that can serve as a touchstone when considering the impact of various decisions.

# 14

# RACE, ETHNICITY AND MEDICINE

If you were to peek inside your medical chart, you might notice that one of the things that is recorded is your race or ethnicity. In fact, when doctors communicate with one another, the opening sentence will read something like this: "Mrs. X. is a forty-year-old Chamorro woman," or "Mr. Y. is a seventy-year-old Filipino man." If you were the suspicious type, you might exclaim, "Hey, what's up with that? Are the doctors discriminating against me?"

Race and ethnicity are important pieces of information for medical reasons. Diseases occur differently in different age groups, sexes, races and ethnicities. By mentioning sex, age and race in the opening sentence, entire groups of diseases can be excluded and others come to mind.

For example, I received a letter last week that said, "Mrs. S. is a fifty-two-year-old Carolinian woman who has double vision." A study we published years ago showed that if you are a Carolinian woman in the CNMI in your fifties, you have a fifty percent chance of having diabetes. So, the immediate thought that comes to my mind is to test Mrs. S. for diabetes. (Diabetes can cause small strokes to the nerves that control eye movements thereby causing double vision.)

Likewise, some diseases such as multiple sclerosis are found mostly in Caucasians, specifically those of Scandinavian descent. It doesn't mean that you can't find multiple sclerosis in another race. It just means that the chances are lower. Tumors of the eye and skin called "melanomas" almost never happen in those of us that are darkly pigmented. Melanoma is a disease found almost exclusively in light skinned people. So, if I see a dark spot on someone's arm, the diagnostic considerations are completely different depending on whether that person is Caucasian or Chamorro, because the Chamorro has genetic protection.

Sickle cell anemia occurs in people of African and Mediterranean ethnicity. If I read a medical chart and it says "Mr. T. is an eighteen-year-old Chinese man with bleeding inside the eye," I don't even consider testing for sickle cell anemia. But if I read that "Mr. T. is an eighteen-year-old African-American man with bleeding inside the eye," testing for sickle cell anemia will be high on my list.

Diseases also behave differently because of genetic differences. For example, glaucoma, which can be a blinding condition in anyone, is particularly aggressive in African-Americans. It needs to be followed more carefully and treated more aggressively in that population.

Mentioning age, sex or race and ethnicity in a medical chart is not an indication of discrimination. These demographics help guide your healthcare professional to the appropriate diagnosis and help us understand how your disease might behave.

# 15

## MEDICAL EDUCATION

I was happy to meet young Felix Cabrera a few weeks ago. Felix arrived home to Saipan after completing his first year of medical school. He is here to undertake some research with the Department of Public Health during his summer vacation. It's always encouraging to see new local talent coming into the medical profession. It's clear that we need more indigenous physicians returning home to the CNMI to serve the community. Young people often ask me what it takes to become a doctor. Here is a brief summary.

First of all, you need to go to college. Under most circumstances, you'll need to complete a bachelor's degree. Although some universities offer a "pre-med" major, this is rare. You can major in anything you want, and still be well prepared for medical school. Generally, you need to take one year of general chemistry, organic chemistry, physics, calculus and biology. Beyond that, you can take any classes you want and major in anything that you want. In fact, medical schools look very favorably upon people that come from majors like art history, or literature or music. They like to see candidates that are well-rounded and who can relate well to people. As an undergraduate, one of my majors was the History and Literature of Religion. I pursued a course of study that was interesting to me, and it was one of the things that helped me get into medical school.

During the undergraduate years, you need to get good grades – lots of A's, some B's, maybe one or two C's. And no D's or F's unless you've got a really good reason. You don't have to master every subject you ever study in order to be a good doctor, but being a good doctor requires the ability to rapidly digest large amounts of information. Medical schools think that good grades are a sign that you can handle information.

About a year before going into medical school, you'll have to take the MCAT, or "Medical College Admission Test." The test covers the science and math courses and examines your ability to comprehend and interpret data. The better your score, the more likely you are to get into medical school.

After your four years of university and a bachelor's degree, you start medical school. Traditionally, the curriculum includes two years of classroom work, followed by two years of clinical work. The first year is spent learning the way a normal body works, and the second year is spent learning about the abnormal body and diseases and their treatments. The third year is then spent almost exclusively taking care of patients in a hospital, under close supervision. There are core services that one rotates through during the third year – typically three months each of surgery, internal medicine, pediatrics and obstetrics-gynecology. The fourth year is also a clinical year, but it's a chance to take some electives. I remember that during my fourth year I spent a month on the plastic surgery service, a month on the neurosurgery wards, a month doing pediatric infectious disease work, and a month in the emergency room, dermatology, neurology, ophthalmology (my favorite) and rural medicine.

Medical education has changed some since the time I graduated in the late 80's. Now you may spend more time with patients as a first year student, and also instead of spending one year on the normal body and the next year on the abnormal body, you'll spend a month on different systems. For example, you'll spend a month studying the heart – the normal heart, the abnormal heart, the treatment for various heart conditions, and even get to see some patients with heart conditions. Many schools are now using this "systems" approach or "problem-based" approach.

After four years of medical school you're a Medical Doctor – MD. But you still can't practice medicine. You need more training. If you want to become a pediatrician, you'll need to spend three years in a pediatrics "residency." During this time, you are again working under the supervision of more experienced doctors to take care of patients and learn about a particular specialty. This is one of the purposes of the electives you take during the fourth year of medical school – to help you decide what specialty you want to enter. The big six are family practice, pediatrics, surgery, internal medicine, obstetrics-gynecology, and emergency medicine. There are also specialties like neurology, psychiatry, dermatology, radiology and ophthalmology that you can enter. Many of these specialties require one year of general training and then three to four years of specialty training. For example, I did one year of internal medicine training as part of my training in ophthalmology.

So far you have four years of university, four years of medical school and three, four or five years of a residency (depending on the specialty) under your belt. Believe it or not, you still might not be finished. Although at this point you can go out and work as a full-fledged specialist, many doctors choose to go on to get even more specialization. They will do a "fellowship" – extra years to become a sub-specialist in their field. For example, after five years of a surgical residency, you decide you want to become a heart surgeon – that's five to seven more years. Or after three years of an internal medicine residency, you decide to become a pulmonologist (lung specialist) – that's three more years. Each major specialty has bunches of subspecialties that require more years of training.

Felix has gotten his bachelor's degree and a year of medical school under his belt. He's got at least three more years of medical school and three years of a residency ahead of him, and perhaps a few years of sub-specialty training before coming home for good. It may seem daunting, but no matter what, the time will pass.

# 16

## WHAT IS YOUR DESTINY?

Last Saturday night, I, along with some 200 other people at the Hotel Association of the Northern Mariana Islands' (HANMI) 20th Anniversary Dinner witnessed a rare moment.

It has been said that the whole secret of success is to discover your destiny, and then fulfill it. Each of us has a unique set of gifts and talents. Our whole purpose in life is to hone these unique attributes, no matter how great or small they may be, and to use them in service to others. Many of us do indeed develop skills that we use for the benefit of humanity. Whether we are spending the majority of our waking hours as a doctor, teacher, mother, clerk or carpenter, we are contributing to the advancement of civilization. Many of us absolutely love what we are doing. But I think that many of us wonder if we are doing what we were created to do – if we are fulfilling our destiny. And this, I believe, was what was so enthralling about last Saturday night. We witnessed a young man fulfilling his destiny.

Those of us attending the HANMI dinner had received the invitation that read, "With Music by Jake Shimabukuro,

Master of the Ukulele." Now, most of the time, when the word "master" is used, I envision someone weathered by time – maybe someone in their sixties or older – I think of Master Yoda.

So it was a bit of a shock when "Master" Jake walked out with spiked hair, a faded T-shirt and jeans, looking barely old enough to shave. I thought he was the guy who comes out first to check the microphone. You could hear people saying, "He's just a kid!"

Jake began to speak, and with that the magic began. He thanked HANMI and its Chairwoman, Lynn Knight, for the invitation to come to Saipan; he spoke of his experience with the children's ukulele band earlier that day; he spoke with genuine warmth and intensity, and you could feel that even if the music were to end up being crummy, here was someone who loved what he was doing. He remembered the names of everyone he'd met that day.

Jake pulled up a chair and began to perform. His fingers created such rich sounds that I imagined they were coming from a full orchestra, not a little four-string instrument that until that night the uninitiated considered a sort of small toy guitar. For the next ninety minutes, we were all mesmerized. But I believe that it was not just because of his amazing technique. I think that the most moving part of the experience was being witness to a person doing what he was created to do. We watched a young man fulfilling his destiny. He was not just a great performer. Watching him play was like watching creation. The music flowed through his every expression. He connected with heart and soul to those around him. He expressed such pure enjoyment at each new change in the music, as if he were being taken by surprise by the sounds emerging through his hands. You got the feeling that *he* was the instrument, and that some force was playing him. It was hard to imagine someone doing anything in the world any better, or enjoying it any more. It was moving to watch.

I contemplated how fortunate one must be to have found one's destiny. I thought about my own four children and my hope that they might discover their gifts in the same way, and uncover their talents so that their lives contribute to the maximum extent to humanity. I also began to wonder how our educational system might change if it were focused on one task above all others: helping each child discover their unique destiny. The experience gave me cause to pause and wonder if I were fulfilling my own destiny. I thought of the words of composer Bernice Johnson Reagon, as sung by *Sweet Honey in the Rock*,

> *My God calls to me in the morning dew.*
> *The power of the universe knows my name.*
> *He gave me a song to sing and set me on my way.*
> *I raise my voice for justice. I believe.* [12]

May we all find our song, and sing it boldly. Thank you, Jake, for letting us watch.

# 17

## SEVEN REASONS
## NOT TO MESS WITH A CHILD

These seven reasons were sent to me by a friend. The author is unknown (at least to me). They're sure to help start the day with a smile.

One. A little girl was sitting and watching her mother do the dishes at the kitchen sink. She suddenly noticed that her mother had several strands of white hair sticking out in contrast on her brunette head. She looked at her mother and inquisitively asked, "Why are some of your hairs white, Mom?" Her mother replied, "Well, every time that you do something wrong and make me cry or unhappy, one of my hairs turns white." The little girl thought about this revelation for a while and then asked, "Momma, how come *all* of grandma's hairs are white?"

Two. A Kindergarten teacher was observing her classroom of children while they were drawing. She would occasionally walk around to see each child's work. As she got to one little girl who was working diligently, she asked what the drawing was. The girl replied, "I'm drawing God." The teacher paused and said, "But no one knows what God looks like." Without missing a beat, or looking up from her drawing, the girl replied, "They will in a minute."

Three. The children had all been photographed, and the teacher was trying to persuade them each to buy a copy of the group picture. "Just think how nice it will be to look at it when you are all grown up and say, 'There's Jennifer, she's a lawyer,' or 'That's Michael, he's a doctor.'" A small voice at the back of the room rang out, "And there's the teacher. She's dead."

Four. A Sunday school teacher was discussing the Ten Commandments with her five and six-year-olds. After explaining the commandment to honor thy father and thy mother, she asked, "Is there a commandment that teaches us how to treat our brothers and sisters?" Without missing a beat one little boy (the oldest of a family) answered, "Thou shalt not kill."

Five. The children were lined up in the cafeteria of a Catholic elementary school for lunch. At the head of the table was a large pile of apples. The nun made a note, and posted it on the apple tray, "Take only *one*. God is watching." Moving further along the lunch line, at the other end of the table was a large pile of chocolate chip cookies. A child had written a note, "Take all you want. God is watching the apples."

Six. A teacher was giving a lesson on the circulation of the blood. Trying to make the matter clearer, she said, "Now, class, if I stood on my head, the blood, as you know, would run into it, and I would turn red in the face." "Yes," the class said. "Then why is it that while I am standing upright in the ordinary position the blood doesn't run into my feet?" A little fellow shouted, "'Cause your feet ain't empty."

Seven. A little girl was talking to her teacher about whales. The teacher said it was physically impossible for a whale to swallow a human because even though it was a very large mammal its throat was very small. The little girl stated that Jonah was swallowed by a whale. Irritated, the teacher reiterated that a whale could not swallow a human; it was physically impossible. The little girl said, "When I get to heaven I will ask Jonah." The teacher asked, "What if Jonah went to hell?" The little girl replied, "Then you ask him."

# 18

## A NEW KIND OF ELECTION

As we complete the final days of our election year, I realize that almost everyone has distaste for partisan elections. We hate not only partisan politics, but also the actual election process which pits one person against another (or against three others). It's a difficult process to be a part of. After all, the human spirit is drawn toward kindness, compassion, and peace. The current system of elections does not support these values. A political campaign is a war. Either defeat your opponents, or die politically. Fighting is not a happy state for anyone. At the end of any campaign, the candidates typically call for unity, simply because the process itself is so divisive and wounding. Deep down, the world has grown tired of the whole partisan politics election process. But we don't know any other way. Perhaps it is time to recognize that the party system, while having served the needs of democracies for years, is not conducive to the kinds of relationships and communities we need to build into the future.

Is there a better way to elect leaders? What could be changed about the electoral process that would maintain a democratic system designed to select individuals that are well suited for leadership, while also maintaining the unity of the community?

Over the past two decades, old governments have crumbled and new countries have risen up. As these fledgling nations were faced with creating their constitutions, the United Nations drew their attention to a unique and refreshing system of elections that could serve their nations well. As far as I know, none of these new nations adopted this new system of elections. Perhaps it seemed too radical, too unfamiliar to accept. I wholeheartedly believe, however, that during the next century this new system of elections will be adopted by communities and nations, weary of the political war we now wage.

In this proposed system, there are no candidates. That's right. No candidates. There are no nominations. And there is absolutely no campaigning. At every level of government, from the village on up to the national (and even international) level, people would quietly go to the polls on election day, would be given a ballot that simply lists the position, for example, "Governor" or "Mayor" or "Two Senators," and would write the name of any voting adult that they think is best qualified to serve in the particular position. There would be no candidates' names on the ballots, because no one is specifically a candidate. Everyone is effectively a candidate, because every voter is eligible to be elected to office. As a voter, your conscience would guide you. These simple steps, in themselves, bring forth many people who would have no interest in running for office, but who are well qualified to serve.

The process, though not adopted by any government, is in place and does work in many communities and groups around the world today. The key to its success is to refrain from naming individuals, from voicing one's own desire to be elected and from discussing one's intended vote. Thus, the unity of the community is maintained, and individuals elected have the obligation to assume their posts as an act of service and duty to their communities. But it takes a disciplined, restrained and selfless electorate for this system to even begin to work.

In such elections, money is not spent on campaigns, consultants, strategists, rallies and all the rest. No one criticizes anyone else. No one is disenfranchised as a result of the election results. In fact, no one is "running." Anyone duly registered to vote can be elected.

This system may sound crazy at first, especially in light of the culture of competition that we have grown used to. I suspect it will take many years for us to evolve to the point of being able to institute this system at a governmental level, but does it not sound more consistent with the values of the human spirit? At the very least, is it not a system that can be adopted by our community organizations – our clubs and schools and boards and civic organizations?

Thinking of our current system of elections, I am reminded of one of my favorite quotations that extols the virtues of change:

> *"If long-cherished ideals and time-honored institutions, if certain social assumptions and religious formulae have ceased to promote the welfare of the generality of mankind, if they no longer minister to the needs of a continually evolving humanity, let them be swept away and relegated to the limbo of obsolescent and forgotten doctrines. Why should these, in a world subject to the immutable law of change and decay, be exempt from the deterioration that must needs overtake every human institution? For legal standards, political and economic theories are solely designed to safeguard*

*the interests of humanity as a whole, and not humanity to be crucified for the preservation of the integrity of any particular law or doctrine."*[13]

Let us view our current system of elections as a step along the journey of humanity's social evolution. It has served us well. But it is becoming increasingly clear that eventually we will implement a better way — a way more in keeping with the aspirations of the human spirit.

# 19

## IF YOU AND I MEET ON NEW YEAR'S EVE...

If you and I meet for the first time on New Year's Eve, chances are that you'll soon be asleep. I'll be wearing gloves, peering through an operating microscope, carefully passing sterile needle and thread through your ruptured eye. Nearly every year, around the holidays, I am in the operating room, sewing together someone's eye that has been blown to bits by fireworks.

Fireworks are a leading cause of injuries during the holidays, and eye injuries account for around one out of five fireworks-related injuries. Unfortunately, because of the devastating explosion, blindness usually results from a fireworks injury. Most of the time, it is a bystander that is injured.

In reality, there is no truly safe way for non-professionals to use fireworks. Many states ban fireworks, or at least, the most dangerous kind – bottle-rockets. In Australia there is an almost complete ban on the sale of fireworks, without much detriment to the "fun" people experience in celebrating the holidays. The American Academy of Ophthalmology, the American Academy of Pediatrics, and the American Public Health Association all advocate banning the sale of fireworks, because of the dangers posed by them.

The organization, Prevent Blindness America, keeps track of various statistics related to fireworks injuries. According to the organization, sparklers, firecrackers, bottlerockets and Roman candles account for the vast majority of fireworks-related eye injuries. Almost half of all injuries are to children under fifteen years old. Even sparklers, which are common at birthday parties, can be dangerous since they heat up to over 1800 F – hot enough to melt gold, let alone an eyeball.

It is not always the person using the fireworks that gets injured. Data from the United States Eye Injury Registry shows that bystanders are injured much more commonly than the fireworks operators themselves.

If an injury does occur, what can you do to minimize its effects? First of all, keep in mind that the eye has probably been ruptured by the injury, and as such, the contents of the eye can be further lost. One of the goals is to prevent the stuff that belongs inside the eye from squishing out of the eye. So, you must avoid putting any kind of pressure on the eye. Do not touch the eye or rub the eye. If you can, try not to even squeeze your eyelids. Any of these actions can cause further bleeding or can squeeze the contents out of the eyeball. You can protect the eye from further pressure by holding a foam cup over the eye.

You don't want anything to come out of this open eyeball, but you also don't want anything to go into it either. So, do not rinse the eye or splash it after a fireworks injury. Also, do not place any eye drops or eye ointment into the eye.

The primary task is to get to an emergency room as quickly as possible so that the eye can be examined and treated. The eye will be painful, and it may be tempting to stop for some pain medications, but over-the-counter medicine will not help the pain significantly. Get to the emergency room, and don't stop along the way.

Finally, in most cases, surgery will be necessary. Do not eat or drink anything after the injury, as this can delay the surgery.

The best medicine is always prevention. Children are at high risk, so do not let your children play with fireworks, even if their friends are setting them off. It is often a bottle-rocket that strays off course that injures a watching child. Before you buy fireworks this year, it is worth thinking about the risks. At the very least, do not buy bottle-rockets, or other "shooting" types of fireworks. Ensure that anyone around the fireworks is wearing some kind of eye protection.

Best of all, consider leaving the fireworks out of your celebration all together.

I wish you a happy and safe New Year's celebration. Hopefully, you and I will not ring in the New Year with a suture between us.

# 20

# SUCCESSFUL WEIGHT LOSS

Now that the New Year is upon us, thousands of people around the world have promised themselves to lose those extra pounds. Few will succeed. Already, by the second week of January, many have given up. How about you?

I had a few extra pounds that I was trying to get rid of for years. As I moved through my thirties I began to put on a little extra weight around the middle. I tried everything to get rid of it – increasing my exercise, limiting the number of times I went back to the buffet line, switching from soda to water – but nothing seemed to work.

Then, two years ago, a miracle. I adopted a radical change in my diet, and within twelve weeks I had lost twenty-five pounds and was back down to my high school weight. Within the first three weeks my cholesterol came down from a dangerously high 205 to a very safe 153. I didn't have to exercise much. And I was never hungry. The diet is one detailed in the book *Eat to Live* by Dr. Joel Fuhrman, and it's one that I recommend to anyone who is serious about losing weight or even just adopting a healthier lifestyle.

One of the things that I learned by researching all kinds of diet plans, is that no matter what, you have to change what you're doing now. It may seem like an elementary concept, but I think that we often delude ourselves by believing that we want to lose weight, without really accepting that it will take some change in lifestyle. The other thing that I learned is that it's actually easier to be successful making a radical change in lifestyle, than it is to make minor changes. With minor changes, it's just too easy to slip back.

Why did I like *Eat to Live?* It makes total sense medically. The human body was not designed to go hungry, and any diet that has you hungry is going to fail. *Eat to Live* is not so much a diet as it is a dietary lifestyle. I tell my patients that with *Eat to Live* you can eat as much as you want, as often as you want. But, you cannot eat whatever you want. You will be giving up certain foods, probably some foods that you really like (foods that have made you fat in the first place), but the overall rewards are great. It's based upon eating foods that are high in nutritional value and very filling but low in calories. The first couple of weeks on the diet can be difficult, after all, it's all about change, and change is always hard. But amazingly, the weight just starts to melt away. I really couldn't believe it. Every week I would get on the scale and be shocked to find that the pounds just kept coming off. In those twelve weeks, I lost seven inches from my belly. I was never hungry, and I didn't need to exercise more than twenty minutes every other day. In fact, the whole purpose of the exercise is not so much to burn calories, but to keep your metabolic rate up so that your body doesn't slow down as it tries to conserve its calories.

The best thing about *Eat to Live* is that it actually works. It doesn't require anything fancy. Everything you need is at the grocery store. I've been recommending *Eat to Live* with such success that the bookstore has difficulty keeping it in stock. Let this be the year that you succeed in losing those extra pounds and keeping them off. In three months you could be twenty-five pounds lighter and on your way to a healthier life.

# 21

## S<small>WEET</small> S<small>IGHT</small>

T his doesn't happen often, but this morning after performing my first surgery of the day, I ended up in tears.

About a month ago a gentleman from a neighboring island came into my office, unable to see. When he was a child, he was hit with a rock in his left eye, and that eye had been blind since then. Anyone who has one blind eye is usually vigilant about taking care of the remaining eye. After all, there is no spare, and any problem with the good eye can lead to a lifetime of darkness. If you've already lost one eye, you don't take it for granted that you'll have the other one the rest of your life.

So, like many people with one blind eye, "Mr. Smith" had visited a lot of eye specialists during his life. As he grew older, the vision in his good eye began to grow dim. He was told that he was developing a cataract. A cataract occurs when the lens inside the eye gets cloudy. Usually the cloudiness develops gradually over a number of years. The treatment is a straightforward operation to remove the cloudy lens and replace it with a new clear artificial lens. It's a safe procedure, but like any surgical procedure (or like anything in life) it has certain risks. Although the risks are so very small, they are so very important to someone who has only one eye. Any surgery can result in bleeding or infection, and if these complications happen around the eye, the vision can be lost.

For someone with one eye, that's not a risk you undertake lightly. So, Mr. Smith kept putting off the surgery year after year. After all, he could still see and get around. Why take the risk? But with each passing year, the cataract got a little cloudier, and the vision got a little worse. Finally, he had no choice but to get the surgery. He had gotten to the point that he couldn't see anything but shapes and shadows. He couldn't see well enough to walk safely through a room. This is what life was like for Mr. Smith as his wife guided him into my office. He knew he needed surgery. He was scared. He needed a surgeon to trust. He had visited eye specialists in the region, and had decided I would perform his surgery.

Today I took Mr. Smith to the operating room. When a cataract is as dense as Mr. Smith's, the surgery is quite a bit more difficult and the risk of complications higher. Mix this in with the fact that this is Mr. Smith's only eye, and therefore any complications could leave him completely blind for the rest of his life, and you can see that the stakes are pretty high.

One of the wonders of modern cataract surgery is that the person is awake during the surgery. With the anesthesia, the eye feels no pain but it can still see during the surgery. Mr. Smith is watching the surgery as it's taking place inside his eye. I spend a lot of time delicately removing the pieces of the cataract from inside the eye. It's a tense time. The final pieces of the cataract are removed. The riskiest part of the surgery is over. The next step is to put the artificial lens into place. The lens will bring the world into focus. I carefully guide the artificial lens into the eye, and feel relieved. The surgery takes place through an incision so small that it doesn't even need stitches. We're done. Everything has gone very well. I move the operating microscope out of the way, and no one is quite prepared for what happens next. Mr. Smith softly says, "I can see." He lifts his head and looks around, and says again, with more excitement, "I can see!"

Of course, the reason we do the surgery is to help someone see, but sometimes we forget how dramatic it can be for someone who has been in darkness for years to suddenly see again. The members of the operating room team look at each other with a sense of satisfaction. By now Mr. Smith is exuberant and is shouting, "I can see! I can see! I can't believe it! I can see! I can see your shirt! I can see your face! I can see the colors!" And as we're wheeling him to the recovery room, we're all getting choked up by his excitement and he keeps saying, in amazement, "I can see!"

I walk out to the waiting area to let his wife know that everything went well. The problem is that by now, my eyes are full of tears and I can hardly talk. Mrs. Smith takes one look at me and I see horror on her face. She sees the tears in my eyes and must think I'm coming to tell her that things didn't go well and that her husband is blind forever. I realize I need to talk quickly, but I can barely speak. I manage to choke out three words: "He can see." Those are sweet words to a woman who thinks I'm coming to break bad news. She jumps up and half screams and half asks "He can see?" She jumps for joy and now both of us have tears streaming down our faces.

It's nice to feel the sweetness of someone else's joy once in a while – to become aware of the miracles that take place every day around us, sometimes close, sometime far. And to remember the things that we take for granted, like sight, can be so dearly missed by others and so deeply cherished.

# 22

## RELIGIOUS SUPERIORITY

The news of the bombing of the Golden Mosque in Iraq, and the reprisals and deaths that have ensued seem to give a glimpse of a force that could completely destabilize that already suffering country. It is not a force that is unknown to humanity, having given rise to rivalries and wars that have claimed thousands of lives down through the ages. It is the force of religious and sectarian hatred, which finds its roots in ideologies of religious superiority.

Religious and sectarian hatred is a strange but common phenomenon. In the last few days in Iraq, we see members of two sects of the same faith out to destroy one another. The Sunnis and the Shiites both recognize Muhammad as a manifestation of God, but disagree on secondary matters. It calls to mind similar sectarian wars among the followers of Christ. In Europe Catholics and Protestants, both recognizing the divinity of Christ, but disagreeing about various aspects of the message, have spent centuries in tense confrontation which, even to this day, continues. Religious hatred also takes an inter-religious form, and at any given moment in the history of humanity the followers of one faith have been out to eliminate the members of another.

The underlying problem is not a difference of belief. After all, we all have differences of belief about all sorts of things. The problem is the idea that "my belief is better than your belief." The problem is the conviction of one's own superiority – religious superiority.

Religious leaders have done much to strengthen the faith of their followers and to inculcate codes of behavior, ethics and morality. Yet it is religious leadership that bears primary responsibility for engendering attitudes of religious superiority. The sometimes open, but often subtle, proclamation that "we are better" that rises from pulpits (even here) is the kindling that prepares a society to capture the sparks that ignite a religious conflagration.

It is odd that in this day and age, where ideologies of superiority of race, sex and national origin have been relegated to the fringe elements of society, the idea of religious superiority is an unquestioned tenant of our lives (even here). The underlying principle that unseated these other ideologies of superiority was the recognition of the principle of the oneness of humanity – that despite our secondary differences with regard to race, nation or sex, we are fundamentally one people and are intrinsically equal in the eyes of a loving Creator.

The parallel principle that must be unequivocally embraced and proclaimed by the world's religious leaders in order for religious hatred to end is the principle of the oneness of religion. One international institution has written: *"The time has come when religious leadership must face honestly and without further evasion the implications of the truth that God is one and that, beyond all diversity of cultural expression and human interpretation, religion is likewise one."*[14]

As long as religious leaders nurture ideas of religious superiority in the minds of their followers, they nurture the conditions under which hatred and bloodshed are allowed to emerge. It is the religious leadership that can most rapidly put an end to ideologies of religious superiority. It is the ideology of religious superiority that leads to fanaticism and intolerance and fuels the fire of religious strife.

# 23

# A SNEAKY THIEF

Baseball Hall of Famer Kirby Puckett's untimely death this year brought to mind the day in 1996 when he announced his early retirement from the sport. He had awoken one morning in March with blurred vision, and by the end of that season, had retired. What happened? What caused Kirby Puckett, who led the Minnesota Twins to win two World Series, to leave the sport he loved? What kind of disease can make such a thing happen?

The disease is glaucoma. It is the leading cause of preventable blindness in the United States. And it is on the rise here in the CNMI. There are two scary things about glaucoma. First, you can have it for many years without even knowing it. It causes damage slowly and gradually over time, with no symptoms at all. Glaucoma steals your sight away from you. That's why it's often called "the sneaky thief of sight." Second, the damage is permanent. Once glaucoma causes loss of vision, you cannot get that vision back – not through glasses or medicine or surgery or laser or diet or anything. Glaucoma causes permanent loss of vision. It's the sort of disease you want to pay attention to.

The good news is that the damage from glaucoma can be prevented, but only if you know you have glaucoma and get it treated. In fact, glaucoma is the main reason that the American Academy of Ophthalmology recommends that adults get an eye exam even if they have no vision problems at all: once during your 20's; twice during your 30's; and then every few years during your 40's and above. Glaucoma may be slowly, relentlessly, painlessly causing permanent damage to your eyes right now. You won't know it. You can't even recognize the damaging effects, because glaucoma attacks the peripheral vision. A gradual loss of peripheral vision is difficult to notice. When you finally do notice it, there will hardly be any vision left. It will be lost forever.

Who can get glaucoma? Anyone. But there are some people who are at higher risk. If someone else in your family has glaucoma, it puts you at higher risk. (My grandmother lost her vision to glaucoma, so I'm at risk.) If you have diabetes, your chances of having glaucoma are higher. And if you are African-American, you are at high risk for glaucoma. Yet there are plenty of people who are Chamorro or Filipino or any ethnicity, who have no family members with glaucoma and who don't have diabetes, but who walk in for an eye exam and are found to have glaucoma. Any of us could have glaucoma and not know it.

The goal is to find glaucoma early, before it has stolen much of the sight. When glaucoma is caught early, medications can prevent further damage. Having glaucoma doesn't mean you will lose your vision. Finding glaucoma early means you can keep your vision healthy for your entire life. Glaucoma can be controlled with medications or other treatment. It needs to be monitored regularly.

Knowing all of this, you can understand how glaucoma snuck up and stole Kirby Puckett's sight and ended his career. It could happen to any of us, and might be happening to you right now. Find out. An eye exam can be the first step to catch this "sneaking thief of sight," and help you keep your vision for life.

# 24

## Putting Winning Aside

We all face choices every day. This story was given to me by my friend and co-worker, Russ Quinn. The author of the story is unknown. It's a story about choices and the goodness in the world.

ɷɷ

At a fundraising dinner for a school that serves learning-disabled children, the father of one of the students delivered a speech that would never be forgotten by all who attended. After extolling the school and its dedicated staff, he offered a question:

"When not interfered with by outside influences, everything nature does is done with perfection. Yet my son, Shay, cannot learn things as other children do. He cannot understand things as other children do. Where is the natural order of things in my son?"

The audience was stilled by the query.

The father continued. "I believe that when a child like Shay, physically and mentally handicapped, comes into the world, an opportunity to realize true human nature presents itself, and it comes in the way other people treat that child." Then he told the following story.

Shay and his father had walked past a park where some boys that Shay knew were playing baseball. Shay asked, "Do you think they'll let me play?" Shay's father knew that most of the boys would not want someone like Shay on their team. But the father also understood that if his son were allowed to play, it would give him a much needed sense of belonging and some confidence to be accepted by others in spite of his handicaps.

Shay's father approached one of the boys on the field and asked if Shay could play, not expecting much. The boy looked around for guidance and said, "We're losing by six runs and the game is in the eighth inning. I guess he can be on our team and we'll try to put him in to bat in the ninth inning."

Shay struggled over to the team's bench, put on a team shirt and a broad smile. His father had a small tear in his eye and warmth in his heart. The boys saw the father's joy at his son being accepted. In the bottom of the eighth inning, Shay's team scored a few runs but was still behind by three. In the top of the ninth inning, Shay put on a glove and played in right field. Even though no hits came his way, he was obviously ecstatic just to be in the game and on the field, grinning from ear to ear as his father waved to him from the stands. In the bottom of the ninth inning, Shay's team scored again. Now, with two outs and the bases loaded, the potential winning run was on base and Shay was scheduled to be next at bat.

At this juncture, do they let Shay bat and give away their chance to win the game? Surprisingly, Shay was given the bat. Everyone knew that a hit was all but impossible because

Shay didn't even know how to hold the bat properly, much less connect with the ball.

However, as Shay stepped up to the plate, the pitcher, recognizing that the other team was putting winning aside for this moment in Shay's life, moved in a few steps to lob the ball in softly so Shay could at least be able to make contact. The first pitch came and Shay swung clumsily and missed. The pitcher again took a few steps forward to toss the ball softly toward Shay. As the pitch came in, Shay swung at the ball and hit a slow ground ball right back to the pitcher.

The game would now be over, but the pitcher picked up the soft grounder and could have easily thrown the ball to the first-baseman. Shay would have been out and that would have been the end of the game.

Instead, the pitcher threw the ball over the head of the first-baseman, out of reach of all teammates. Everyone from the stands and both teams started yelling, "Shay, run to first! Run to first!" Never in his life had Shay ever run that far, but he made it to first base. He scampered down the baseline, wide-eyed and startled.

Everyone yelled, "Run to second, run to second!"

Catching his breath, Shay awkwardly ran toward second, gleaming and struggling to make it to second base. By the time Shay rounded toward second base, the right-fielder had the ball. The smallest guy on their team, he had a chance to be the hero for his team for the first time. He could have thrown the ball to the second-baseman for the tag, but he understood the pitcher's intentions and he too intentionally threw the ball high and far over the second-baseman's head. Shay ran toward second base deliriously as the runners ahead of him circled the bases toward home.

All were screaming, "Shay, Shay, Shay! All the way, Shay!"

As Shay reached second base, the opposing shortstop ran to help him, turned him in the direction of third base, and shouted, "Run to third, Shay! Run to third!" As Shay rounded third, the boys from both teams and those watching were on their feet screaming, "Shay, run home!" Shay ran to home, stepped on the plate, and was cheered as the hero who hit the "grand slam" and won the game for his team.

That day, said the father softly with tears now rolling down his face, the boys from both teams helped bring a piece of true love and humanity into this world.

Shay didn't make it to another summer, and died that winter, having never forgotten being the hero, and making his father so happy, and coming home and seeing his mother tearfully embrace her little hero of the day.

# 25

## SECONDHAND PEE

I've always known that my sense of humor at times is so subtle as to be obtuse. I was reminded of this by the feedback I received on my column, printed three weeks ago, on secondhand pee. Two general categories of responses to *Secondhand Pee* came in: those that loved the column and thought it was a hilarious commentary on secondhand smoke (about ten percent); and those that thanked me for informing them that certain pools have peeing-sections, noting that from now on they would be careful about where they swim (about ninety percent). So, I need to set the record straight. There are no pools with peeing sections. Tourists have no particular penchant for peeing in pools. The column was in fact about secondhand smoke. It started with the quotation, *"Having a smoking area in a restaurant is like having a peeing section in a swimming pool,"* which established the context of everything else that followed. Because it is a ridiculous idea that a pool would have a peeing section, it is equally ridiculous for a restaurant to have a smoking section. Some apparently small number of people got the joke of the column. They recognized that the very absurdity of presenting a serious argument against peeing in the pool highlights the equally absurd notion that we consider it remotely okay to smoke in a restaurant. I was hoping to capitalize on this absurdity. I do admit that my wife, Mara, warned me that I was being too subtle.

So, here is the column again. Any time you see "pee" think "smoke," and when you see "swimming pool," think "restaurant." I'll probably have to permanently cap my comedic pen. It's never a good sign when you have to explain your jokes before even telling them, just so more people will recognize the punch line. Ah, the unhappy perils of having an obtuse sense of humor! Let me know if it's any better the second time around.

❧

Before I start let me say that I hope I won't terribly offend your sensibilities by what follows. My hope is to shed light on a subject that should be obvious, but seems to have gotten obscured by a lot of smoke. Sometimes you gotta take a chance to help people see things from a new perspective. Here goes.

*"Having a smoking area in a restaurant is like having a peeing section in a swimming pool."*

It's a pity that swimming pools here have not instituted a non-peeing policy. Health officials are now considering the idea of banning peeing completely from public places. Over the past few years government offices have gradually adopted and implemented a policy of peeing only in designated areas. I do hope that our islands' businesses soon voluntarily adopt policies that ban peeing from all public places, including swimming pools.

The issue of peeing in swimming pools is a touchy one. The argument has been presented that by banning peeing from swimming pools, our tourists will be upset. The practice is common in their home countries, so the argument goes, and if we implement a non-peeing policy, our tourism will be adversely affected. After all, a nice relaxing pee along with a cup of coffee after a swim is an integral part of the swim. How can you possibly enjoy a swim when you're denied the pleasure of peeing in the pool afterwards!

In reality, tourists know that they are in a foreign land and are prepared to suffer all kinds of inconveniences, like using weird looking money, hearing strange accents, and even being denied the pleasure of peeing in a foreign pool. If they've traveled before, they expect that here too, the swimming pools will be "pee-free" and that pools will not have a special peeing section.

For years, those who have not been inclined to pee in the pool – the "non-pee-ers" – have been working to enlighten folks about their perspective. They have argued that peeing in a pool just isn't a nice thing to do. It's, well, somewhat foul. You go into a pool expecting a nice swim, and leave tainted by secondhand pee. People simply don't like being exposed to secondhand pee. But recent scientific studies have shed new light on this subject. The issue isn't just that exposure to secondhand pee is unpleasant. It's downright dangerous. Research has shown (not surprisingly) that secondhand pee is a risk-factor for all kinds of disease. It increases cancer, heart disease, and a variety of other problems, especially in children who are exposed to secondhand pee.

Banning peeing from public places, particularly swimming pools, is not an issue of restricting the rights of pee-ers or of stepping on the toes of our tourists. It's a matter of common sense and good health, backed by real scientific data. Secondhand pee is bad, not just unpleasant. I do hope that if you are a swimming pool owner, you don't wait for official policy to remove the peeing section from your establishment. Make your restaurant smoke-free ... um, I mean, your swimming pool pee-free. After all, where would you rather swim?

# 26

## FIGHT BACK

O pening an email is a jarring experience these days for those of us who care a whit for the written word. Put a perfectly literate person behind a keyboard, ask him to respond to an email, and suddenly all signs of literary convention are sucked out of his head by that glowing screen. He types, and it's just a stream of letters joined to make words joined to make ideas rarely joined to make actual sentences just strewn across the ephemeral electronic page. It's rare these days to receive an email with a salutation, a hint of capitalization, or a sprinkling of appropriate punctuation. What is going on?

It's easy to get overly relaxed with email. There is something about the medium that isn't as serious as picking up a pen and paper and formulating one's thoughts. There is an intrinsic informality about email. But it's gone too far, I say, too far! I now routinely get email, from highly educated people, mind you (teachers even!), that lack a single capital letter, and that have these weird contracted abbreviated words ("ur" instead of "you're"). There is not a single apostrophe or period to be found. And forget about anything that resembles a "Sincerely" or "With best regards" at the end. Email is ushering in the death of written literacy as we have known it. Legions of email senders (I won't call them "writers"), sit low in their chairs, typing along, "wooohooo! look at me! im so relaxed im not using any standard writing conventions what about u? isnt this email thing gr8."

I suppose the argument is made that by skipping these conventions of the written word, one saves time, speeds up the process. By golly, that message needs to move out of here in a flash; people are waiting for it; it's gotta fly; it's gotta get back out there! Who has time for a bunch of superfluous conventions when this message before my face is hurrying me to send it? There is not time to type "Dear Harriet." Can't be bothered with the *shift* key in this race against an unseen clock. These electrons might miss their ride, so there's not time to close the door with a "Fondly yours," as it rushes out, barely clothed (how embarrassing for us all). It'll do fine. It'll find its way. Just get it out there without a nanosecond of wasted keystrokes, and then take a break and relax. So the thinking goes, I suppose.

Maybe that reasoning makes me feel better, but what about all those messages I get that weren't written with any self-imposed sense of urgency? What about that message from my buddy, Joe, that I know is typed late at night, while Joe is sitting in his pajamas (maybe), eating chips? I know he's not even sitting up straight in his chair. I know he's not in a hurry. He's never in a hurry.

I open the message, and the first words to strike my incredulous eyes are not "Dear David," or "Hello David," or even a friendly but universally impersonal "Yo Dude." The email just dives in: "hope ur doing well. im fine" I rub my disbelieving eyes and realize I should be grateful that there is at least one punctuation mark in the email. Yes, I concede that it's a single period shared between two sentences, but one punctuation mark is far better than none.

But the "ur" just jars me. Any brief consolation I got from that lonely period evaporates under the burning heat of "ur." There it is, sitting in the very first words: "ur"... "ur." It's unsightly, like seeing a bit of food fly out of someone's mouth while they're talking. Tolerable, but a sight from which you want to politely avert your gaze, pretend not to notice. While in your head, ah, in your head, you shout a visceral, instantaneous, "Gross!"

I ask myself, "What in the world is this guy doing that he can't type those three extra letters and an apostrophe to make a proper word, 'you're'?" After pondering this question for a while, the answer comes to me. It arrives in a flash. I can explain it: he's typing with his toes! Of course! Silly me! I realize he probably isn't eating chips after all. He is eating a plate of very large and messy barbeque ribs. Needing two hands to handle the sauce-drenched ribs, he has resourcefully taken off his socks, plopped his feet onto the keyboard, placed his hairy-knuckled toes on the keys most appropriate for efficient foot-typing, and away he goes. That explains it, because when ur typing with ur toes, u must conserve keystrokes. Go, Joe!

But then my mind turns to the complete and glaring absence of uppercase letters. What's that all about? After all, you can still get some capital letters into the email if you're typing with your toes. Press the *shift* key with one pinky toe, and use the big toe of the other foot to simultaneously press the desired capitalized letter. It's not too difficult. So what gives?

Ah, then I realize, in another epiphany: it has nothing to do with the dripping ribs! Joe has been struck by a terrible temporarily paralyzing disease – an epidemic striking email senders around the world. Oh, the humanity! While at a keyboard, the sufferers can barely move. There's poor Joe, pecking out letters, one at a time, slowly, deliberately, with one of those long pointer antennae-like thing-a-ma-bobs strapped to his head with a leather belt. Poor fellow's probably in a lot of pain straining his neck to reach the *q*. There are beads of sweat on his upper lip. Of course, the primitive gizmo doesn't allow even those who yearn deeply to capitalize their *i*'s (as Joe must, I'm sure) to do so; it does not allow one to simultaneously hold down two keys. It's a one-key-at-a-time piece of technology.

A sad scene, but hey, I'm happy because, *voila*, I've solved the puzzle. Now I can explain why I get these emails with no uppercase letters. I'm compassionate. It must be frustrating to a breaking point, to be one of the millions of email send-ers suffering from this insidious plague. Unable to use their hands or feet to type while at a keyboard, they peck peck peck one letter at a time, with no hope of ever regaining the full use of their *shift* key.

But what about the apostrophe? His email lacked even an apostrophe! Confound it! My theory is shattered, because even a single pigeon-like head peck could have placed an apostrophe in its proper place, restoring a modicum of self-esteem to that sad, permanently lowercase "im."

What are we to do, we who give a hoot? How can we combat this flight, this exodus, this banishment of the marks of literacy from what has become the most common form of written communication, the email. Fight back with resolute action, I say! Sit up straight at the computer, pull that uni-antennae off your head, put two hands on the keyboard, raise your wrists like a concert pianist, and make full and resolute use of those combinations of keys that are beginning, from disuse, to become unrecognizable to you. Boldly place a salutation at the beginning of the email! ("'Tsup, George!") Sign off descriptively and with pride! ("Your ever-abiding servant, Buford.") Shift every *i* to an *I*, standing tall! ("*i* am *I*, hear me roar!") Use apostrophes for contractions and possessives! ("It's cool.") Envelope those weird loner letters with their natural complementary partners, healing and transforming the isolated ones into gregarious letters, a part of living words! ("You're going to love the change.") We can do it. We shall overcome this blight upon the screen. Nothing can stop us. I'm thrilled, just thinking about the possibilities... i hope u r 2.

# 27

# I ♥ Heroin

About once every year, I'll succumb to the temptation of processed meat. I'll buy a can of it (not entirely guilt free), plop the quivering mass onto a plate, slice off a few quarter-inch slabs, fry them gently in a pan, place them tenderly on white bread (what would be the point of using wheat?), cover them with a thin sheet of mayonnaise, slowly savor each bite, and schedule my cardiac angiogram.

Heroin, on the other hand, I've never actually used. But one time I got to use one of its relatives. And man, was it dangerous. In my case, the heroin and the can of meat happened within hours of one another, so it was truly a memorable day.

It was about four years ago. That afternoon I had my annual fix of canned meat – white bread and all. By evening I went to bed with a mild stomachache. I awoke in the middle of the dark night, writhing in pain, balled up in a knot. Being a doctor, I knew right away, as most doctors know when they have something seriously wrong with them, that I was just fine, no problem, not sick, nothing can touch me. That kind of thinking in the face of unquestionable severe personal illness is common among doctors, and I wasn't about to break with tradition. I tried to ignore the searing pain and go back to sleep. But my whimpering woke my wife, and as a result of her level-headed insistence, I reluctantly got dressed and drove myself to the hospital.

It was an interesting drive. At the time, my daughter was two years old and my son, five months old. If you're already in pain, you don't want your kids sitting next to you in an emergency room screaming, "Why did you wake us up in the middle of the night to drive us to a cold fluorescent room to watch you get worked over. Why are we here? You're a horrible father!" So my wife stayed home with the sleeping kids and I drove myself to the hospital, clutching my abdomen (that's a medical term) and using my chin to deftly control the steering wheel. Luckily, there was little traffic, and I kept control of the car by repeatedly saying to myself, as I always do when driving with my chin, "It's just a video game. You'll get there fine."

When I was getting close to the hospital, I had the presence of mind to call the emergency room to say, "I'm coming in. Don't make we wait. I'm dying." I arrived, was immediately rushed in and assessed to be in very serious condition and was politely given a cardboard number and a ream of forms to complete. I knew I was in pretty bad shape when I heard one of the nurses joke, "Gee, he's looking like one of Jerry's Kids." Ha ha, I thought.

I just wanted the pain to stop. But when you walk into a hospital complaining of pain, if the doctors make the pain go away too quickly, they can't figure out what's wrong with you. So they'll poke and prod you for a while, pressing really hard on your belly then suddenly letting go (that's called "rebound sign" because if you're in pain, you'll leap from the table and out-rebound any 7'2" basketball player that may be hanging around the ER looking for a pick-up game). A special refrigerated abdominal stethoscope quantifies the volume of your screams. Such tools and techniques are all part of the science of medicine.

After a thorough hour of this, the exam is completed. My blood has been taken, x-rays done, the IV is in my vein, and yes, dear, I said the painkiller is on its way.

Heroin is the mother of all painkillers. (Actually, heroin is the daughter of the mother, which is morphine, but let's not get too deep into the family tree.) I got one of heroin's relatives, Demerol. Usually, Demerol gets injected into your muscles. But in my case, I suppose the ER staff wanted to quiet me down quickly, and they mercifully shot the stuff straight into my vein. With one heartbeat the bolus flowed from my arm to my heart. And with the next beat, those Demerol molecules went screaming gleefully to the pain relief centers of my brain. The Demerol crashed into the receptors, and faster than I could say, "Hey, where's my body?" all pain ceased. Stopped. Nothing. Gone without a trace. I was floating.

Having never used any kind of recreational drug, I now understood why people use the word "high." I floated around the room doing slow-motion summersaults, the backstroke, cool Ninja moves, giggling; all the while watching myself sleeping peacefully on the gurney. I was thinking, "Wooooohooooo, so this is what drug abuse is all about! Now I get it! Oh, man, I'm going to become a junkie for a living."

One shot, and I was an addict. As I continued my travels over my bed, the lab results and x-rays came back showing that nothing serious was wrong. (I didn't hear that.) I was admitted to the hospital for observation, "just to be safe." (I didn't hear that either.) The doctor was so kind as to tell me that if I had any more pain, "Just let the nurses know and they'll give you some more Demerol." (Baby, I heard *that!*) "And, oh, lunch tomorrow is processed meat." Could it be true? I had already had both in the same day, and now the opportunity for more? I felt alive!

When I returned to my body and awoke the next morning, the struggle for my soul began. The conversation with myself went something like this.

"Hey, ask for some more Demerol. You're not in pain, but no one has to know that. After all, pain is relative. Compared to that high, just existing, breathing, thinking is painful. Ask for another shot of that stuff. Come on!"

"Dude, you can't do that. You'll never leave the hospital. You'll taste it again and then you won't be able to stop. They'll be on to you and throw you out into the street with the back of your gown untied. And then you'll be coming back every day faking pain just to get some more of that stuff."

"So? At least get one more shot of it. Just one more shot! It's there for the asking. This is your last chance. If you don't, you may never get it again. You can always check yourself into the Betty Ford Clinic later."

After half an hour of this conversation, I started to scare myself. I was a junkie just waiting to happen. That's some dangerous stuff. All the while I'm holding a parallel conversation in my head as to whether or not to eat the processed meat that was coming for lunch. That's some dangerous stuff too. I ended up getting "scared straight" and didn't ask for either, not that day, not ever again. After two days, I was discharged from the hospital with a diagnosis of "non-specific gastritis," which is sophisticated medical terminology for "tummy ache — we have no idea why."

What does any of this have to do with anything? Who knows. But I do know that heroin and processed meat both make you feel great (at first). But used regularly, sooner or later, either will kill you. And the processed meat addict is in much worse shape, what with no readily available detox centers here on island, or in Honolulu, Guam or Manila. It's something the Community Guidance Center may want to explore. Or maybe some private investors. Until then, be careful out there, and don't re-use forks.

# 28

## ORGANIC SMOKE (AND MIRRORS)

An hour before my previous column was to be printed, I received a call from my editor, Jayvee. "David, I can't publish this column as written." This must be bad, I thought. Did I offend someone? Was it because I used the word "heroin"? Or worse, did I make some unforgivable grammatical error? Jayvee quickly informed me that the problem was with a certain four-letter word that appeared in the column. He would have to replace the word. The word that I had used starts with *S* and ends with *M* and rhymes with *Pam*. The replacement phrase that appeared in the edited final version of the column was "processed meat."

What's going on, I asked Jayvee. Why can't I use the word that starts with *S* and ends with *M* and rhymes with *Pam?* Can I use *Something Posing As Meat* instead? Or how about *Scientifically Produced Animal Matter?* As it turns out, this minor hubbub occurred because one of the other columnists had made mention of this infamous processed meat brand that starts with *S* and ends with *M* and rhymes with *Pam* in a disparaging way (though I'm not sure that is possible) and Jayvee had received a friendly letter from the lawyers of the corporation that makes the processed meat brand that starts with *S* and ends with *M* and rhymes with *Pam*, saying, in effect, "Stop making fun of us, or we'll sue your pants off."

Apparently, these folks don't want any attention drawn to the implications of the nutritional label on the side of their product. Total calorie count: 609 (for a small seven ounce can). The label clearly points out that nearly eighty percent of the calories in every mouthful come from fat. This is not a nutritional food. *Calorie-Count.com* gives it a nutritional grade of D+. If anyone draws your attention to the fact that the product is not a great one, the lawyers come knocking. They get really upset if we're doing it in a humorous way.

What gives? Well, sometimes the obvious needs to be stated. There are forces in the world that work very hard to influence you, and that do not have your best interests in mind. They have their own best interests in mind, and in the case of some private enterprises, those interests usually have something to do with separating you from your money. You would think that in this day and age of health consciousness, any respectable, well-intentioned company that makes a product of such lousy nutritional value would somehow conclude, "You know, this was a good idea during the War when people needed fat-in-a-can with an indefinite shelf-life. But in today's world of rampant obesity, what's the point? Let's just pull it off the market."

I know, I know. That's a naïve dream from some kind of ethical world where "market forces" are not the god at whose altar all excuses are lain. But the point is, as consumers, we have to realize that there are indeed forces out there that do not have our best interests in mind. In fact, those forces may not give one hoot about our best interests. I've recently been flabbergasted at the boldness of a new advertising campaign that strives to make a particular brand of cigarettes seem healthy. Their advertisements, which appear in all kinds of magazines, invoke ideas of patriotism and the natural spirit of the Native Americans. They tout their tobacco as being "natural" and even go so far as to point out that it is "organically grown." Organically grown! That's outlandish temerity. Stick the word "organic" next to anything, and everyone automatically associates it with being good for you. Heck, just toss a pack into the grocery cart right next to your soy milk and alfalfa sprouts and enjoy! They're *organic* cigarettes.

The tiny print in the ad clearly states "Organically grown tobacco is no better for you than any other tobacco, and in fact, tobacco causes lung cancer, death, low-birth weight, vision loss and pretty much any avoidable disease you can think of, but we're going to do everything possible in this ad to keep your attention away from these words. Don't look at the little black-and-white Surgeon General's warning box. Look over here at all these pretty colors. And at this hot babe beckoning you to come share a smoke."

The list of institutions, be they private or public, that do this sort of, well, *lying*, under the euphemisms of "marketing" or "public information" is long. As you become attuned to the process, you can recognize it, and reflect a bit about what is being done to influence you. It's worth taking some time to ask, "Is this really good for me? Is this really what I want?" because sometimes, no one else will ask on your behalf. Bring on the *organic* version of that processed meat that starts with *S* and ends with *M* and rhymes with *Pam*. We'll be ready.

# 29

## FIGHTING RISING CRIME

O n Sunday, a friend of mine took his family down to Micro beach to enjoy a day in the water. They parked on the side street by the Hyatt and walked over to the beach. After a few hours, they headed back to their car, and what should they see but a young man using a metal rod to try to break into their family car. It was a surprising scene. It was broad daylight, in a fairly busy area, and here is a guy in full view of traffic, hotel security cameras and anyone walking by, trying to jimmy the lock open.

"Hey, man, what are you doing?"

"Nothing."

"Well, it doesn't look like you're doing nothing. It looks like you're trying to break into my car."

"No. I'm just cleaning it for you."

"Cleaning it? Thanks. Do I owe you some money for that?"

"No. Actually, there were two guys trying to break into your car, but it's okay now. I ran them off and I called security for you."

"Really? You called security?"

"Yeah. Everything's okay."

"How did you call security? You have a cell phone?"

"No. Everything's cool, man," says the thief, extending his hand for a friendly shake.

When my friend refused to shake his hand, the fellow must have realized that his story wasn't going to sell on this sunny day, so he jumped into his blue sedan which he had parked right next to my friend's car. As he pulled out to make his escape, my friend said to him, "I've got your license plate number, buddy. ABC-503. You can run, but you can't hide." In one of life's beautiful ironic twists, on the back of this young thief's car was a bumper sticker for Crime Stoppers.

People often say that the crumbling economy is the cause of rising crime. I agree that it may be a driving force for rising crime, but it's not the root cause. I believe the cause is a crumbling morality. Crime and misconduct are not controlled effectively by a healthy economy or by a strong police force. Just take a look at all the recent crimes of corporate millionaires or the murders happening every day in countries where troops try to keep order in the streets, and it becomes clear that the most effective deterrent to crime is not wealth or force. The most effective deterrent is a strong sense of personal morality. Some call it conscience. Some call it fear of God. Some call it a healthy sense of shame. Whatever you want to call it, it is this quality that maintains orderly conduct and civility in the face of dire pressures to succumb to our animal and materialistic impulses.

When I think of crime prevention, I think of it in much broader terms than locking windows, buying alarms, lighting neighborhoods and increasing patrols. These certainly are helpful, but ultimately, the solution is to teach rising generations of children the moral imperative to live honest lives, even if it pains them.

We can look to the guidance offered in all the world's religions, because religion, at its foundation, is all about motivating individuals to change their behavior and to bring their actions into conformity with certain divine precepts. Religion helps set standards which purely humanistic philosophies cannot do. Yet at the same time, I do not think that we should leave moral education – or what some may feel more comfortable calling "character" education – solely up to religion. I see no reason why schools cannot develop curricula that teach a child the importance of truthfulness, honesty, integrity, kindness, humility, courage and all the rest of the human virtues. I would like to see crime stopping organizations, whether public or private, implementing broader crime prevention methods that seek to address the heart of crime: character.

As part of my religious education, I was required to memorize this passage:

> *"They who dwell within the tabernacle of God, and are established upon the seats of everlasting glory, will refuse, though they be dying of hunger, to stretch their hands and seize unlawfully the property of their neighbor, however vile and worthless he may be."* [15]

That's a pretty broad mandate that leaves little room for one's conscience to justify even a teensy-weensy bit of theft. Even if you're dying of hunger, don't do it. Even if your prospective victim is vile and worthless, don't go there.

One of the things that rankles some people about religion's motivational forces is that religion is often linked with encouraging fear or shame. Relax. There is nothing wrong with a healthy sense of fear or shame. In fact, the lack of such traits leads to the sorts of "shameless" behavior of a young man trying to break into a car in broad daylight, and then staying around to chat about it, even shake hands over it. A sense of shame will serve him well. It will protect him from his own impulses. Without it, he remains who he is.

The cause of crime is not poverty; it's a lack of morality. It's not lack of force; it's a lack of character. Address these issues, and crime can be prevented even on the darkest loneliest street.

# 30

# HYPERBARIC OXYGEN CHAMBERS

Tomorrow night marks the gala event in this year's celebrations of the 20th Anniversary of the Commonwealth Health Center (CHC) Volunteers. If you haven't made plans yet to attend the fundraising dinner, consider joining the festivities at the World Resort tomorrow evening.

Over the years the CHC volunteers have done much to enhance healthcare on the island and to improve the quality of each patient's experience at CHC. Their current goal is an ambitious one, and one that will have a far reaching impact. They are raising funds for a hyperbaric oxygen chamber. What is this and why is it so important to you?

A hyperbaric oxygen chamber is a hard shell vessel where oxygen can be administered at pressures higher than atmospheric pressure. The chambers come in various sizes, and can hold from one to eight people at a time. Hyperbaric oxygen chambers have two important functions – one related directly to the oxygen and one to the pressure.

A hyperbaric chamber allows more oxygen to be delivered to the body than is possible at normal atmospheric pressure. At pressures above atmospheric pressure (that is at "hyper-baric" levels), more oxygen is pushed from the air into the body and delivered to tissues. At normal atmospheric pressure, even when breathing 100% oxygen, the red blood cells become saturated with oxygen and the blood quickly reaches a maximum carrying capacity for oxygen. However, at higher pressures, the red blood cells become saturated, but oxygen can now also move into the fluid (or plasma) of the blood. Therefore, more oxygen can be delivered to the tissues of the body than is possible at normal atmospheric pressure.

This is important primarily because more oxygen can help wounds heal faster. This isn't too big of an issue in people with normal wound healing abilities, but it can make a big difference when wound healing is compromised. If there is already a problem with blood and oxygen flow to a particular tissue, as is the case in someone with diabetes, then wound healing can be a big problem. In fact it is this difficulty with blood flow that results in the non-healing and infected wounds that affect the feet of many diabetics. These non-healing wounds or ulcers can eventually lead to amputations. Placing such a person in a hyperbaric oxygen chamber helps these wounds heal, and can prevent amputations. That's great news for the CNMI's 4000 diabetics.

The second important use of a hyperbaric oxygen chamber is related to the pressure itself. Decompression sickness, which occurs when divers ascend too quickly and nitrogen bubbles form in the blood, is treated by placing the diver in a high-pressure chamber. The nitrogen bubbles are dangerous because they can become large enough to block the flow of blood. When blood flow is blocked, say to the brain, the person suffers a stroke. In other areas such as joints, nitrogen bubbles can lead to pain. The high pressure in a hyperbaric chamber allows the nitrogen bubbles to dissolve back into the blood and to leave the blood gradually, without forming risky bubbles.

The presence of a hyperbaric chamber greatly enhances the CNMI's ability to attract divers. Many divers do not consider traveling to an area that doesn't have a hyperbaric chamber, because a chamber can make the difference between life and death. A hyperbaric chamber will place the CNMI in that category of premier dive destinations. In addition to offering outstanding dive sites, we will be equipped to handle one of the most dangerous diving risks, decompression sickness. And that's good for everyone.

# 31

## Beautify CNMI & Hope

I believe we're all inspired by high ideals. *Beautify CNMI* is an inspiring group. Every week or so this group of volunteers sets out to beautify some area of the CNMI. It's a simple idea that comes from love of one's home, pride in one's land, and a desire for beauty. It is these sentiments that inspire me. *Beautify CNMI* is a grassroots movement that welcomes everyone to join in.

On a deeper level, *Beautify CNMI* is about much more than just cleaning up our islands. Every faith looks to a day when human beings will live lovingly with one another and when civilization will not be the mess that we see around us today. It may seem a distant dream, but I have hope when I look around the world, because there is clearly a dual process taking place. There is a process of disintegration whereby various segments and institutions of society are falling apart, and there is a process of integration whereby new ones are being built. The disintegration manifests itself in much of the horror we see around us, the convulsions of dying ideologies. So, yes, the world is falling apart, but I see it as a required process of movement toward a better world.

Parallel to this process of disintegration, there is a clear process of integration taking place. If you look for it, you will see it. We see people arising to work together. We see old barriers to human relations coming down. We see science moving us toward a global community, requiring the recognition that we are inhabitants of a common homeland, one in spirit. And we see grassroots movements around the world tapping into the roots of human motivation to better their communities. *Beautify CNMI* is a part of this integrative process that uplifts humanity.

Their work is divine work because they are engaged in the work of beauty. I see any process that seeks to add beauty to the world as "symbolic of the nature of the transformation which is destined to occur both within the hearts of the world's peoples and in the physical environment of the planet."[16] *Beautify CNMI's* work is symbolic of that transformation destined to occur.

Congratulations to one of the planets integrative forces, *Beautify CNMI.* Today is a big day for them. Their goal has been to have 1020 volunteers by October 20th. (Get it? 1020 by 10/20?) They have exceeded 3000 volunteers. Hooray for all of us! Today and tomorrow, you may see *Beautify CNMI* volunteers undertaking an island-wide beautification project. In the midst of the chaos and rubble around us, if you look, you can see the forces at work that are moving the world toward its sublime destiny. *Beautify CNMI's* work is not just about picking up trash. It's a symbol of transformation. It's about inspiring hope.

# 32

# THANKSGIVING DIET

As we round the corner toward Thanksgiving, people want to know, "How should I approach the holiday to remain healthy?" You'll hear health gurus saying "watch your portions, eat vegetables, avoid fats and sweets," and all the rest. But not from me. I say, eat whatever you want! As much as you want! Go ahead! It's Thanksgiving for heaven's sakes! Eat, enjoy, indulge, celebrate! Gulp down the whole turkey! Consume only apple pie and ice cream if you want! No need to restrain yourself and put a damper on your day! Eat! Eat! Eat! After all, it's only one day a year, right?

You see, if you are healthy, what you eat on one day of the year isn't going to make a big difference to your health or to your weight. So, I say, enjoy yourself. The real question is, what are you doing on all the other days of the year? Are you treating every day like Thanksgiving, stuffing yourself until you're in a food induced torpor, engorged like a plucked tick? If you are, it's those other 364 days of the year you need to work on. So let's talk a little about those other days of the year and what you're doing to your body.

First of all, let's get an idea of how healthy you are. Take a tape measure, preferably a cloth or plastic one like a tailor uses. Wrap it around your belly right at your belly-button. What's the measurement? Studies have shown that the simplest risk for heart disease is this measurement, the "umbilical girth." Regardless of your height or your build, if your umbilical girth is over 40 inches, you're at high risk for heart disease. Below 35 inches starts to decrease your risk, and 30 inches or less is ideal. If you're more than 30 inches, Thanksgiving is not your problem. The other days of the year are what will kill you. If you don't have a tape measure handy, just take a pinch at your navel. Can you pinch more than an inch? If so, I'm sorry to report, that the extra weight puts you at increased risk for heart disease.

Losing weight is a miserable endeavor. The human body simply was not designed to give up its stores of energy (also known as fat). You have to wrestle every calorie away from it. No matter what diet you follow, there are two themes that will keep coming up. First, you'll have to give up something. You cannot keep eating the same things and expect to lose weight. Yet at the same time, a diet that leaves you hungry is doomed to fail. Your body is designed to eliminate hunger, and you will… by eating. Now, I'm going to tell you a secret. You can actually eat as much as you want, and still lose weight. The secret is, you cannot eat whatever you want. Got it? Eat as much as you want, but not whatever you want. Naturally, the question arises, what are the foods that I cannot eat in this "as much as you want" diet? You cannot eat fat and you cannot eat carbohydrates. So, limit the amount of oil (fried foods) and animal products, which are where most of our fat comes from. And limit the amount of carbohydrates – bread, rice, pasta, potatoes, cakes, cookies, sweets, soft-drinks and beer – ideally to just half a cup per day. That's half a cup per day *total*. You can eat as much fruits and vegetables as you want. Eat twenty oranges in a day if it strikes your fancy. Eat ten heads of lettuce if you like. You will not be hungry, and you will lose weight.

The second theme that comes up in any diet you examine is that you do actually have to exercise. This is in part so that you'll burn more calories, but there is a more important reason. When you start to lose weight, your body senses the loss, and reacts. "Hey, what's going on here? We aren't supposed to give up these stores of fat. We need them for survival in a famine." And the body, in response to the loss of calories, lowers its metabolism. It slows down so that it doesn't burn calories as quickly. It goes into a conservation mode. So, you need to battle this slowing metabolism, and you can do this through exercise. It doesn't take much. Vigorous aerobic exercise, as little as 20 minutes three times a week, helps trick your body into keeping its rate of metabolism up or even increasing it, so that you can keep burning calories and losing weight.

Now, I must give you a warning about totally indulging yourself on Thanksgiving. This is fine if you are *not* overweight, and do *not* have diabetes, hypertension or heart disease, or any other health problems. If you have heart problems (and you may not even know you do), it is dangerous to over eat, even one meal, because eating takes blood to your stomach and away from other vital organs like the heart and brain. If your heart is already strained, a heavy meal can take valuable blood away from it. In fact, heart attacks often come after a heavy meal. And, of course, with diabetes, you cannot take in too many calories because of the risk of skyrocketing blood glucose which can lead to a coma.

Enjoy your Thanksgiving and spend your effort on making every day of the year a healthy eating day.

(I thought I had already finished writing this piece, but such is the state of the world that I'm required to say: This information is provided for general information only. It is not intended to provide medical advice, and should not be relied upon as a substitute for consultations with qualified health professionals who are familiar with your individual medical needs.)

# 33

# THE NEXT 100 YEARS

Wtih the impending implementation of federal minimum wage in the CNMI, and the possibility of federalization of immigration, we are thrown into a speculative turmoil. The air is thick with uncertainty. Businesses brace themselves for the possibility of higher wage-related expenses, and the loss of access to guest workers and their skills. Businesses also brace themselves for the possibility of a massive decrease in the islands' population, and the resulting decrease in business.

As I think about these changes, which are being viewed by many as cataclysmic, I consider the larger changes that we are sure to undergo over the next 100 years. The changes over the past century have been mind-boggling considering the relatively short period of time into which they have been compressed. For example, 165 years ago, the fastest way to move was by horse or by wind. People never imagined moving very far in their lifetimes. Communication likewise traveled at those same speeds. But in a short period of time, advances in science have shrunk the world. Circumnavigation of the globe is measured in hours, not months. Communication with nearly any spot on the earth is possible at near instantaneous speed, and takes place with a device that most people carry in a pocket. Information of any sort is available anywhere. Everything is global. Consumer brands are global, war is global, pop culture is global, disease is global, economies are global, even global warming is global.

We have been brought into contact with one another, and have progressively come to realize that, on a fundamental level, we are all essentially the same. There is a consciousness of the oneness of humanity. We may vary in language, culture, ideas, and shade of color. But only those on the fringes of thought continue to argue for the inherent superiority of any nation, race, or religion – or for the inherent right to privilege resulting from place of birth, ethnicity, language, or cultural heritage. We have come to recognize the principle of the oneness of humankind. I'm convinced that this principle *and its implications*, more than anything else, will guide the changes of civilization (and of the CNMI) during the next 100 years. The implications of the principle of the oneness of humanity are vast. New institutions and mechanisms will be created to express these implications. To the extent that we embrace this emerging paradigm, we will flourish.

If we are going to talk about "brotherhood" or "love thy neighbor as thyself," it requires more than warm fuzzy feelings. It requires creating the institutions that make these principles mean something practical. Primarily, the principle of the oneness of humanity implies the formation of a global commonwealth of nations that are permanently united – a world federal system with a world tribunal, a world legislature and a world executive. It implies organizing the world in such a way that its vast resources are distributed equitably; that opportunity is available to all, regardless of the randomness of one's place of birth.

You may be skeptical that governance on this scale is possible, but already we see significant steps toward a commonwealth of nations – nations who cede some elements of their national sovereignty for the benefit of the whole. The European Union is one such association. The world has lots of experience with willingly combining separate political entities into a unified whole. Two modern examples are the unification of the colonies into the *United* States of America, and the process through which the feudal states of Germany became a nation. The next 100 years will see the further development of the blending of nations into members of a global commonwealth with a global government.

Those member-nations will be citizens of the global commonwealth, and movement among them will be as free as it is now between California and Nevada. California is not overwhelmed by immigration from Nevada, because both states are part of a federation that ensures that citizens of both states have the resources they need (mostly, anyway). So will it be with the members of the global commonwealth. When the CNMI becomes a member of this yet-to-be-born global commonwealth, our borders will be open to other citizens of the global commonwealth, and our labor and immigration will not be locally controlled, or even federally controlled, but rather will operate under the guidelines of the global commonwealth.

In broad strokes, these changes are inevitable. Just observing the forces of history makes me certain of this. Some see such changes as beneficial. Others see them as a utopia – a fantasy. Still others see them as catastrophic, even apocalyptic; a sign of the "end times." I am of the first group. My sense is that as an island community, we will reach our fullest potential only to the extent that we, over the next century, are able to adopt and fully incorporate the principle of the oneness of humanity into our collective consciousness, our hearts, and ultimately our institutions. Let us recognize and consent to this principle. Once we accept it as a guiding principle, let all other practical considerations flow from it. Make practical plans without taking the principle of the oneness of humanity into account, and you ignore the fundamental driving force of social and political evolution for the coming century.

It has been said that by its very nature, unity requires self-sacrifice, and that self-love (or self-interest) is "kneaded into the very clay of man." The practical requirements of the oneness of humanity are usually derailed by self-interest. Whether you define "self" as me, my people, my family, my clan, my ethnic or racial group, my island, my state, my region or my nation, placing the benefit of any of these entities above those of the generality of humanity is simply self-interest. Acceptance of the principle of the oneness of humanity requires setting all of these variations of self-interest aside and adopting a global perspective, cognizant of each member of the human race. Ironically, it is by setting aside self-interest and working to implement the practical requirements of the oneness of humankind that we establish the conditions under which we, the peoples of these islands, will thrive. Be attentive, and you will see that increasingly, the realization of the implications of the oneness of humankind will be the force that defines the direction of change over the next 100 years.

# 34

# THE RELATIONSHIP BETWEEN
# MORAL HEALTH AND A BLIND WIFE

I called our friend Marta to invite her to dinner. Her housekeeper answered the phone. "Good afternoon, this is Mary." I was quite impressed to be greeted with a time-of-day specific salutation and a name. "Hi, this is David. Is Marta home?" "Sorry, Sir. Nothing Marta." Over the years, I've learned that "Nothing Marta" does not mean that Marta has been vaporized. She is simply not home.

Now I am faced with a choice. Should I leave a message, or call back later? What would you do?

I'm feeling both lucky and a little dangerous, so I decide to leave a message. "Could you write this down please?" I ask, realizing that maybe I don't feel as lucky or as dangerous as I first thought. "Nothing pencil. For a while, sir." I listen to papers shuffling and wait for Mary to come back to the phone. "Ready, Sir." "Please write this down and give it to Marta when she returns home." "Okay, Sir. Ready." "Dinner tonight," I say. "Okay, 'Dinner tonight,'" she repeats slowly as she writes it down. "Five o'clock." "Okay, 'Five o'clock,'" she writes. "David and Mara's House." "Okay, 'David's moral health,'" she writes.

Huh? Say what? Did that really happen? Did "David and Mara's house" really become "David's moral health"? I guess it did. This is what can happen when two people with two different native languages try to communicate. I'm fluent in English, and conversant in two other languages. I often miss things, so I know some funny things can happen on the way to mutual understanding. I'm not conversant in any of this region's languages, so I can't quickly switch to Mary's native tongue to clarify things. So we're stuck with English, right here at "David's moral health." What should I do? Keep trying? Give up? What would you do?

I pride myself on my perseverance (i.e. I'm hard-headed), so I decide to keep going. I will say it again, offering some clarification. It never crosses my mind that the clarification could possibly lead to further confusion.

Here I go. "No, 'David and *Mara's house,*' not 'David's moral health.'" "Ohhhh," she says. "David not have moral health?"

Time to change tactics. "Mary, if it's okay with you, I'm going to spell this. Are you ready?" "Yes sir." *"D-a-v-i-d a-n-d M-a-r-a-s h-o-u-s-e."* She repeats each letter as she writes them down, getting it right, except that she adds an *i* to "Mara," making it "Maria."

I should stop, don't you think? But I can't. I'm thinking to myself, there are lots of Maria's on this island. Marta might know a "David & Maria," and could end up at their house for dinner, causing an awkward moment for everyone just because I didn't want to clarify things. There is only one "David & Mara" on Saipan. Best to clarify. And plus, I realize that Mary is going to give a message to Marta about Mara who has morphed into Maria, so surely, by pursuing this a bit further, there is more humor to be had. I keep going.

"Mary," I say, "Mara is my wife. Her name is *Mara* (said slowly and deliberately by me), not *Maria*. Mara has no *i*. "Ahhhh," she exclaims sadly, "Your wife nothing eyes? Cannot see?"

I pause, and realize that I am, in this moment, truly content. I am in the midst of one of those beautiful multicultural multilingual Saipan moments, that make you want to either laugh, or shoot yourself, or if you are fully experiencing the nuances of the situation, both. I offer to call back later, smile, and head off to ponder the pity that Mary must feel for me, my blind wife, and my poor moral health.

# 35

## TIME SLOWED DOWN

First, he saw a flash of light. Then he felt clear fluid on his cheek. Next, the smell of blood. Then darkness and searing pain. Finally, he heard the explosion.

In the Emergency Room, that's how my friend Jeffrey described to me the slow motion of instantaneous events he experienced when the bottle-rocket blew apart his eye. It made sense. The flash of the retina being compressed before the anterior chamber rupturing and spilled its clear contents onto his cheek. Then, the smell of blood from the explosion of vessels and tissues deeper in the eye. Next, the shearing of the optic nerve leading to darkness; and the activation of pain impulses. Then… then finally, the sound wave, slower than both light and electricity, arrived at his eardrums, and he heard the explosion. Like the delay of thunder arriving after the lightning. All within a fraction of a second.

He wasn't using the fireworks. And they weren't being used by kids. He was just one of the adults standing around at a party while everyone "enjoyed" the fireworks. Light. Noise. The smell of gunpowder. Laughter that suddenly goes still.

On an island, where you're the only ophthalmologist, you don't have the luxury of calling in a detached colleague to do the surgery on your friend. I told Jeffrey it was serious. That I would do everything possible to put the pieces of his exploded eyeball back together again. That he would need more surgery later. And that his chances for recovering any vision were slim. He was twenty-one, right out of college, a volunteer teacher at one of the schools. He thought of the life ahead of him without the sight of one eye, and sobbed. He was my friend. I put my hand on his shoulder. It was the first year of my career. I wasn't yet thirty.

He spent the next seven hours under general anesthesia while I pieced together his mangled eye. Microsurgery. Sutures smaller than human hair. I used package after package of 10-0 nylon suture, 9-0 nylon suture, 8-0 nylon suture. "How many stitches," everyone wants to know. Probably a thousand. You just stop counting. Within the first hour I knew his vision was lost, but I didn't have the heart to remove his eye. Better it be taken out at a major medical center where there would be no doubt that everything humanly possible had been done to save that eye.

As the sun rose, I walked out of the operating room into the tropical half-light, drained and exhausted. Before we went into surgery he had given me his parents' phone number. "Call them for me," he had asked. Now it was up to me to break the news to them. I had to pull them out of President Clinton's Inaugural Ball to take the call. They were thankful.

Within a day, they had flown Jeffrey to Manhattan Eye and Ear Hospital, one of the finest eye care facilities in the world. The surgeons called me. They just wanted to talk to the guy who had done more to rebuild an eye than they had thought possible. Then they did what they had to do. They removed Jeffrey's eye and plopped it into a jar.

Jeffrey chose a prosthetic eye for his empty socket. He looks normal. But he wears glasses every waking second of his life. The glasses protect his remaining eye from the frightening possibility of a stray rock, or finger, or shattered windshield, snuffing out his sight. No spare left. A lifetime in darkness.

I'm happy – no, eager – to give up one small aspect of all of my celebrations: fireworks. Their joyful sounds will never be enough to drown out the sobs of a person losing an eye. It's not a common occurrence, but it's not a rare one either. I hear those sobs every single year. Ban the fireworks.

# 36

# SAIPAN DINING ADVENTURES

My friend and colleague, Mark Robertson, and his wife, Bev, have probably eaten in every restaurant on Saipan. They have an adventurous streak, which you must have in order to explore the full range of dining experiences here.

Take for example the time they went back to the new Mexican restaurant. The burritos had been fantastic the first time, so they returned for a "known known." Again, the burritos came smothered in sour cream. But the first bite betrayed the true identify of tonight's sour cream. Not sour cream. What is that taste? It's familiar. Could it be...? Yep. Sure enough. Thick rich creamy white *mayonnaise* glopped on top of that hapless burrito. Yummy. The kitchen was out of sour cream, so the cook used the next best thing – the next white thing – mayonnaise. Makes perfect sense. That's why you just keep eating.

The following week they venture out to a Korean restaurant. They are warmly welcomed at the door with halting English and a sense of excitement that real live Americans are visiting the establishment. This could be a new beginning, a whole new market! Mark and Bev are seated with grace and a flourish at a table for two, a red plastic rose on the white plastic tablecloth. They are given menus.

One of the nicest things about many Asian restaurants is that the menus include photos of the food, which is necessary in this case, because all the writing in the menu is in Korean. But the photos are still not completely helpful to Mark and Bev, because they are only slightly larger than a flattened clove of garlic.

Mark strains to make out the details of the pictures. Bev can do no better. The logical thing to do is to ask the waitress for help – try to get enough of a description from her to make an informed choice. So they begin, and ever so slowly, work their way, item by item, down the menu. The waitress struggles to find words – any words – but particularly words for foods that have no English equivalent. "Is this spinach?" asks Mark, pointing to the picture. "No," says the waitress. "Is it kelp?" asks Bev. "What 'kelp?'" inquires the waitress. "Oh, kelp is like seaweed," offers Mark. "What seaweed?" asks the waitress. "Seaweed is *nori*," explains Bev, drawing on her knowledge of a Japanese word that might be familiar to the waitress. "Ahhhh," says the waitress as her face lights up, "No, not *nori*." "What is it then?" asks Mark. *"Like* spinach," reports the waitress.

Mark and Bev are enjoying their detective work and are quite content to explore the menu in this way. But the waitress, who has never experienced happy inquisitive stateside Americans, must believe that Mark and Bev are struggling and suffering as much as she is through this ordeal to place a simple order.

Eager to bring some relief, the exasperated waitress offers a great solution. "Maybe you go eat someplace else. Maybe someplace that have spaghetti."

In that instant, her suggestion doesn't quite register with Mark and Bev. But after a few seconds, their comprehension catches up with their hearing. Did she really just ask us to leave? To go eat spaghetti? They glance at each other over their menus and try to hold back their laughter.

Undeterred and ever adventurous, Mark and Bev plow forward, asking a few more questions, making a decision, ordering their meals, and enjoying it all. And tonight they have an opportunity to use their recently gained knowledge – to taste everything white to make sure it's not mayonnaise in disguise.

# 37

## THOUGHTS OF A FATHER

H ave you ever wondered what it would be like to wait for a diagnosis of cancer? I now know. Here are my thoughts from the first day this began last week. I think he'll be okay.

ço∞

My son has a 6.5 centimeter lymph node on his neck. Ultrasound shows an 11.4 centimeter spleen – huge, upper limit of normal for an adult, much less for a six-year-old child. Blood work mostly normal, no clear diagnosis, mono test results two weeks away.

Thus the recommendation to biopsy. Look for cancer – lymphoma, Hodgkin's disease, childhood death.

I held him as he screamed yesterday, the needle entering his vein, and I thought, "I hope and pray this is not the beginning." My sweet six-year-old child, so full of life and joy and determination and creativity and enthusiasm and lost in his plans to move up from kindergarten to the elementary classroom.

We'd take him to MD Anderson or Sloan-Kettering or wherever could give him the chance for cure.

Should he be taken from us, such emptiness would be left all my days. For his sister, her life a dance with his, she just two years older, a gaping emptiness. And every day I would talk to his soul beyond, and ask for his intercession on behalf of his father, for strength and patience to make it without him.

I can imagine all this, but in my heart, it has to just be an exuberant immune response to mono, right? Please? How can my child have cancer? Diverse genetic mix, mostly vegetarian diet, clear island air, no carcinogens. It's just not possible.

I try to cut a deal with God: Save my son, let this all be a lump of nothing, make it all smaller, and I promise I will be good. In however many ways that I'm not, I'll be good.

All my personal concerns, various worries, evaporate under the heat of this lump.

I saw my friend of long ago last year at the Hawaiian Eye Conference. "How many kids do you have," I asked. "Two," he responded, "a twelve-year-old and a ten-year-old." "I thought you had twins." "We did. One died two years ago. Lymphoma." He talked of how this trip to the conference was the first he and his wife had been able to take. There was no time to mourn two years ago. "What can you do?" he said. "You've got these other kids that are alive and who need you. They need your love, your presence, your joy and enthusiasm for them. So you bury one child and try to keep moving forward."

The universe and God I do not understand. Suffering and the suffering of the innocent, I do not understand. And at times like this, I don't try to understand, fearing my explanation or theory may just be false placation. It's just the way it is, and there is nothing I can do about it. Will my magical thinking help? Will the universe still respond with "your wish is my command"? Is my son any more important, just because he is mine? Thousands of despondent parents bury their children every day – death by lymphoma, or leukemia, or tuberculosis, or starvation, or war, or murder. And the world just keeps going on. I just keep going on, thinking about me, my concerns, my pursuits, my hopes, oblivious of their pain and the fragments of their broken hearts. Why would I be so special as to receive my request from the universe, from God? I feel reticent even to ask.

Over the last few years when death would come up in conversations (your great-great grandmother died, Duke died, the cat died), Arman has so often said, "I'm scared to die, I don't want to die alone, can you die with me, Dad?" We realized he thinks that the next world is in the ground, somehow related to the grave. "How will we be able to see each other if we get buried in different holes?"

For most of the day, I'm just doing something else. I look up from my work, and wonder what it was that was causing my anxiety? Briefly forgotten. And the knowledge quickly rushes in, pushes the fragile calm out, my tears well up, and I sob.

# 38

## Reading Deprivation

First of all, some follow-up from last week. Our family was touched by the tremendous outpouring of support from the community this past week as we awaited the results of our six-year-old son's medical tests. Everything has turned out okay. The enlarged lymph node and spleen are returning to normal size and there is no longer any concern that it was something serious. Thank you to all of you for your concerns and prayers. This is a wonderful community to be a part of and we feel blessed to call Saipan home.

Now on to this week's column, and the distractions of everyday life.

৯৵

A few weeks ago, I embarked on what turned out to be an interesting experience. I had been working through a book many of you may have heard of: *The Artist's Way*, by Julia Cameron. It's one of the most powerful books I've interacted with. I don't say "read" because it's not really a "reading" book. It's a "doing" book, with weekly assignments focusing on various facets of developing creativity.

The assignment for the week was "reading deprivation." No reading. That's right. One week with no reading at all. No newspaper, no email, no websites, no books, no blogs, no magazines, no brochures, *nada*.

It's just a way to turn off the distractions and to turn inward; to find some inner space, which can be quite scary for some of us. After all, what will I do if I'm not checking my email six times an hour, jumping from website to website, and newspaper to newspaper?

I was looking forward to the week. I set up my email auto-responder and got ready to see what chaos would break loose.

The no-reading week ended, and I was sad to see it go. I actually pulled it off, much to the disbelieving amazement of my friends and family. I went a whole week without reading anything (well, maybe I read a couple of T-shirts as people walked by, but otherwise, I made it.) I probably haven't spent so much time *not* reading since I was five years old.

Here is what I learned. First, most of my reading these days is "incidental" reading, usually online. I don't sit down with a book or magazine and read in long stretches. Reading often serves to fill some snippet of time – an email when I get home, a blog between patients, an article in the newspaper while the bread toasts. I realized how cluttering it all is, like filling every nook and cranny of time with words.

I thoroughly enjoyed the empty space of the week. What did I do with it? I wrote a lot more, but dared not turn on my computer to write – too much risk of wandering into some reading zone. Instead, when writing I used a thing called a pen. I called friends instead of emailing them. While the bread toasted, instead of reading the paper, I watched my two-year-old smear peanut butter on his face. I just sat and thought a fair bit. (And I thought about significant issues like how long do you have to sit and think before you can say you are "meditating.") I looked at pictures. I cooked up an idea for a line of T-shirts. (Where did that one come from?) I was generally much more present, able to silence the beckoning call of the waiting words.

Now the challenge: applying what I've learned. I'd like to stay word clutter-free. I'd like to contain the clutter in a space of time, similar to keeping all the odds and ends in a junk drawer or closet instead of scattered on every shelf and table through the house. I'd like to contain the word clutter, the "junk-reading" to limited periods of time.

It was a great week. It can be scary, but I know that if I can do it, anyone can. I highly recommend trying a week of reading deprivation.

# 39

# PLEASANTLY OUT OF THE LOOP

One of the greatest things about living on a far-away Pacific island is that you can be as "out of the loop" as you want to be, and not be considered weird.

I was back in mainland America this past December for the first time in seven years. The thing that struck me the most was the level of hype that permeated the air. You couldn't help but to breathe it in. There was no escaping the gases of insignificant events that fill the Excited States of America.

There you can't get away from the hype. Here you have to work to find it.

I just came across a list of the most searched names on the internet, and I've never heard of any of them. They are at this very instant (but probably not for much longer) pumping up the adrenaline of much of the world. It's not like I'm living under a rock. My homepage is set to CNN *International*. I know the broad trends of society and civilization – the important stuff.

Here's the list: Ron Paul. (Never heard of him.) Michael Buble. (Who?) Eurovision? (Presumably a band of some sort.) Joost? (Good name for a drink.) Ubuntu? (I'll go with tribe in Africa.) Paris Hilton? (Okay, I've heard of her, but is she still on the radar screen?) Mario Lopez? Bebo? Sorry guys, your fame hasn't yet reached these sandy palm-lined shores.

Have you heard of these names? I did a little research and here's what I found.

Ron Paul is one of the 2008 Republican presidential candidates who has come out strong against the Iraq war.

Michael Buble is a music guy – sings, writes songs, performs, stuff like that.

Eurovision seems to be the European version of *American Idol* – a singing contest.

Joost is a way to use the internet to watch TV "where you want it, when you want it." It hasn't gone live yet, but apparently there is a lot of anticipation.

Ubuntu is a Linux based operating system.

Mario Lopez is a "hot Hollywood star" (according to his website), and one of the stars of ABC's Dancing with the Stars, which pairs Hollywood stars with professional dancers. (I'd never heard of that either.)

Bebo is a MySpace alternative.

Now that I know all of this, I'm no richer a person. I'm happy to remain pleasantly out of the loop.

# 40

# REVOLUTIONARY
# NEW TREATMENT FOR DIABETES

A few times a week, I'm using a revolutionary new drug to treat some of my patients with severe diabetic eye disease. It's a drug called Avastin.

One of the problems with diabetes is growth of new blood vessels (or "neovascularization") inside the eye. The standard treatment for these new blood vessels is to treat them with laser. But sometimes you put in all the laser you can, and the blood vessels still grow. Avastin is a biological drug that neutralizes the molecule that sends the signal for new blood vessels to grow. The molecule is called VEGF, which stands for "vascular endothelial growth factor."

Avastin was developed by Genentech to be given intravenously for treatment of colon cancer. Many cancers rely upon growth of new blood vessels to nourish the cancer mass. Avastin treats colon cancer by interfering with the growth of the blood vessels that feed the cancer.

An amazingly smart (and courageous) ophthalmologist, Philip Rosenfeld MD, PhD from Bascom Palmer Eye Institute, realized that since Avastin blocks growth of new blood vessels in colon cancer, it should also block growth of new blood vessels in eye disease. About three years ago, he injected Avastin into the eye of one of his patients, and the next day, the new blood vessels were gone. That injection has revolutionized the care of both diabetic eye disease and macular degeneration. I met Dr. Rosenfeld earlier this year in Hawaii, and he's one of the nicest, most generous smart guys I've ever met. We've been in touch by email since then, and he's helped me identify some top-notch retinal surgeons in Japan.

Avastin was approved by the FDA for use in colon cancer, but in the US, we're allowed to use a drug "off-label," meaning we can use it to treat conditions for which it was not specifically approved. We just have to let the patient know that it's an off-label use. When Dr. Rosenfeld used Avastin to treat the growth of new blood vessels, Genentech was already working on a drug that would be FDA approved specifically for the eye. The drug is sort of a cousin of Avastin. The company was in the midst of the FDA study phases when Dr. Rosenfeld decided to try Avastin and Avastin worked. Genentech had invested millions of dollars to get the new eye drug through the FDA approval process, only to have their own drug, Avastin, compete with it through off-label use. The cost of the new eye drug: $2,000 per dose (yeah, three zeros). The cost of Avastin per dose: less than $200.

There are many people in Saipan who have benefited from Avastin and this new era of treatment of diabetic eye disease. Many people in the CNMI who previously needed surgery to treat the new blood vessels are being helped by this new class of biological modulators. It's exciting to be on the leading edge of these medical therapies and to be able to offer the newest and best in eye care to the people of our community.

# 41

## My Grandma
## Banoo & Her Yogurt

I got the email from my uncle. My grandmother passed away last night. She was ninety-three years old. Her mother passed away at one-hundred-and-six. So, we expected my grandmother to be around for many more years. When my parents left Iran in the 1960's to pursue the American dream, the family felt I, at a year old, was too young to accompany them, so I stayed in Iran under my grandmother's care. When she delivered me to my parents a couple of years later, she was my mother to me. My earliest memory is of my grandmother and I flying from Iran to America together.

Her life was full, and like the life of everyone in a developing country, it had its share of tragedy, children lost to accidents and illnesses. In midlife, she immigrated with my grandfather to Canada, that great country that welcomed with open arms people from around the world. Canada was her home, and it was there that she passed away last night. Even when she was in her seventies and her mother in her nineties, they would go sweetly together, their big leather purses in hand, to adult English classes, eager to learn. She never became fluent, but she could get by. She kept the habits of the old country. She persistently bargained with any cashier at the Safeway to give her a better price on the fruit she was buying on a given day. And she cooked. When I think of her, she's often standing before a massive pot of bubbling Persian food, the aroma filling the neighborhood, her fingers holding a knife, chopping onions on a well-worn cutting board.

For the past few years, it seemed our conversations on the phone were a series of missed words. Her mind remained sharp, but her hearing a bit far away. I feel closer to her now that her spirit has joined the Concourse that surrounds us.

Her genes will run through the generations of our family, but more importantly we'll remember her for her courage in the face of massive changes, and we'll remember her with the food we eat. Tonight, I'm going to make some of her yogurt. And if you wish, remember my Grandmother Banoo with a prayer and celebrate her rich life with a bowl of her yogurt. Here is her recipe, which I had shared earlier.

Having spent the first few years of my life in the desert of the Middle East, I was two years old when I first saw snow. I woke early one morning and looked out of my grandmother's house to see the land covered with something white. Having never even heard of snow, I excitedly ran through the house awakening my aunts and uncles, shouting "Come everyone, get your spoons! There's yogurt everywhere!"

I grew up with yogurt, though in the Middle East it's eaten differently than in the West. Instead of mixing it with fruit or honey or vanilla, it is mixed with shredded cucumbers or garlic or salt and pepper.

With the price of yogurt on the island now topping seven dollars for a quart, I've heard people talking of buying yogurt makers. My grandmother had a yogurt maker. It was called a pot. All my life I've made yogurt with a simple pot and a spoon. So, if you want to make yogurt, here is how it's done.

It's all based on the principle that yogurt is a live food. It consists of a certain type of bacteria that turns the milk to yogurt. (If that scares you, don't think about it.) My grandmother's way of making yogurt was to pour milk into a pot, boil it to kill everything in it, let it cool down to a lukewarm temperature, put in a couple of spoonfuls of yogurt (the live stuff that will start changing the milk into yogurt), and then let it sit covered in a warm place for about eight hours. Open the pot, and you've got yogurt. It really is that simple. No need for fancy machines and powdered yogurt mixes and all the rest.

You can make as much yogurt as your pot can hold starting with just a spoonful of live yogurt. In fact, typically we would save a spoonful from the last batch of yogurt to start the next one, and in many families, the successive "generations" of yogurt would carry down through the families from year to year and decade to decade. Generations were connected through their yogurt.

Now, if you don't trust grandma's way (or if you just don't want to take any chances) here is the scientific way of doing it. You'll need a candy thermometer, an oven thermometer, milk, and one of those small containers of plain yogurt. This starter yogurt has to be plain, not flavored. Pour the milk into a pot, and heat it to 180 F. Then let it cool down to 110 F. This may take a long time, so a quick way of cooling it down is to put the pot into a cool water bath (but make sure you don't get any water into it). Once it's cooled down to 110 F, put in two or three tablespoons of the starter yogurt. Now cover the pot and put it in a place that's about 110 F, and that will stay at that temperature for the next eight hours. This is the prime temperature for yogurt to grow. In my house, if I just click the oven to "on," it gets to about 110 F. Another common trick is to just turn on the light in the oven and put the pot in the oven, leaving the light on for the next eight hours. Most oven lights generate enough heat to keep the oven at 110 F. I've also made yogurt by balancing the pot on top of my computer monitor, a nice warm place.

If you want to make the yogurt a bit thicker, while the milk is heating up, stir in about ⅓ cup of powdered milk per quart. More will make it even thicker and creamier.

After eight hours, take a look and you'll see that the milk has been transformed into yogurt. It will be warm, so place it in the refrigerator for a few hours. Many people like to start the yogurt in the morning, put it in the refrigerator in the evening, and then the next morning it's cool and ready to eat. At this point, you can add whatever you want to it – fruit, cucumbers, jam, or other flavorings.

You can make a quart of yogurt this way for the cost of the milk and the cost of a couple of spoonfuls of yogurt. The small cup of yogurt that you bought as the "starter" will last through quite a few batches of yogurt. Or you can save a spoonful from one batch for the next, but despite the stories of generations connected through their yogurt, sometimes the batch loses its potency with time. All in all, it comes out to about $1.50 per quart. Enjoy! But don't try to ski on it.

# 42

## How to Eat Out with Kids and Keep Your Dignity

We were traveling and staying with friends who are first-time parents. Their child is two – the same age as our youngest. For those of you who haven't gone through it yet, let me tell you, the first kid is a shock to the system. It's stressful trying to figure out the workings of a baby and adjust to frazzled sleepless nights. The thought of ever having more than one of these critters is incomprehensible to the first-time parent. At that point in your life you cannot imagine that some day you may look back and think, "One kid was eeeaaasy." When a few more kids come along, you'll think, "One kid? That was hardly stressful!" After our second child was born, I realized how simple it was to just have one. When people would ask me about the transition of going to two kids, I would respond, "One kid is a hobby."

Nevertheless, our friends, like many first-time parents, were frazzled. I introduced them to the idea of how to eat out, and they were so liberated by this simple concept.

The reason it's hard to eat out with young kids is that they don't sit still, and they don't like to wait. The eating part isn't so bad. It's the waiting-for-the-food part that leads to mayhem and beaded sweat on your upper lip. So, Mara and I long ago came upon a simple solution: we place the order from home.

We have the menus of our favorite restaurants at home, and when we do want to go out to eat, one of us becomes the waiter and collects everyone's order. We call the restaurant, and place the order. The restaurant inevitably asks "Will this be for take-out or delivery?" and we say, "We're eating there. We're coming with kids, so we want to have the food ready when we get there." They understand. They are soooo thankful. After all, they don't want our kids sitting idle for twenty minutes waiting for the food to arrive, because, well, they won't be sitting idle. They'll be shooting spitballs, making toothpick forts, spilling water, torturing one another by looking at each other, dropping silverware, wasting napkins, and commenting way too loudly about the wads of chewing gum stuck under the tables. So the restaurant loves that we call ahead. We walk in, they whisk the food out as we pull out our chairs, we eat, and go home with minimal disruption to anyone's sunny disposition.

That's all. Nothing earth-shattering. Very easy. Call ahead and order so the food is ready when you get there. It's a way to reclaim your dignity... sort of... or maybe not really. After all, you're still carrying a diaper-bag and wearing a "dad badge" – that patch of dried drool on your shirt.

# 43

# THE COMMUNITY'S
# UNTAPPED RESOURCE

A friend of mine recently asked me to think into the future and come up with a vivid image of the ideal community. What will be the Saipan that will emerge from the crucible of changes we are going through? Vision helps define our path, and the more clearly we can define our vision, the more chance we have of actually getting there. One of humanity's guiding pieces of literature, the *Book of Proverbs*, states, *"Where there is no vision, the people perish."*

As I began to think about the ideal community, I realized that my initial thoughts are not related to our industries or our economy or our landscape. My primary thoughts focus on our most important resource, a largely untapped and latent resource: the human beings that populate this land. I find it far more appealing to live in a place where the people are vibrant, than to live in a land where all the infrastructure is developed, and the economy is booming, but the people are not.

I realized that I had gone through a similar exercise about seven years ago. At that time, I was involved in creating what we hoped would become a world-class school. We sat down and defined the vision of the institution. We didn't focus on the buildings and grounds and income. Our vision was focused on imagining the type of people we wanted to emerge from the school. And even then, we didn't ask, "What do we want our kids to be when they grow up?" We asked, "What do we want our kids to be *like* when they grow up?"

And so again, as I ponder the future of the Commonwealth, I think that we need to focus our vision on the people. What do we want to be like? As we sat at a table defining the vision of Brilliant Star School, we all tried to imagine our children as adults. If they were in a room full of other adults, what would we want them to be like? What were our hopes for them? We distilled all the thoughts and images into four key qualities.

As I thought about my friend's challenge to imagine the ideal community, I realized that in my mind these same four qualities will define the vibrant person of the Commonwealth. There really is nothing to prevent us from excelling as a community, to be a global showcase of vibrant people. We have developed many vibrant individuals who personify these four qualities, but the untapped potential is vast. The only limitation placed upon us is in our own minds, and our failure to visualize the possibilities. Now, as we are swept up in profound changes, we have the opportunity to define our vision for the one resource that will define the future of the Commonwealth more than any other – the people. A vibrant people will naturally develop an economically and ecologically vibrant community. But by focusing first and foremost on economic fixes, we are placing the cart before the ox. It's time to think primarily of the people, and to define a vision of what we will be like as individuals and as a society.

Here is my vision of the four defining qualities of the people of the future Commonwealth. They are the same four qualities that define the vision of Brilliant Star School.

*Global Understanding.* We recognize that the world of the $21^{st}$ century is one of increasing interdependence among peoples and nations of the world. We recognize the fundamental truth of the oneness of humanity – that all people are one. Our policies derive from this reality. We are comfortable as "world citizens," with a global perspective and understanding of issues. We are free from all forms of prejudice – race, national origin, ethnicity, language, economic status and religion. We recognize the equality of the sexes, and we celebrate the diversity of the world's peoples and cultures. We are promoters of unity.

*Exemplary Character.* We recognize that ultimately, the strength of one's character is the essence of one's self. Character is that set of virtues that are developed in an individual. We have developed, foremost among our virtues, truthfulness, trustworthiness, kindness, courtesy, compassion, confidence, joyfulness, enthusiasm and humility. We are emotionally and spiritually well-developed.

*Service to Humanity.* We recognize that meaning and happiness come from selfless service to others. We strive to find ways to serve others – our friends, families, neighbors and co-workers, our community, and humanity as a whole.

*Creative Minds.* The creative mind is one that can bring knowledge to bear on new situations and challenges. To this end, we are well-versed in the branches of knowledge, with emphasis on mathematics, literature, science, history and arts. We have learned to independently investigate reality, to seek intelligently, and to discover things for ourselves.

We practice applying this body of knowledge and this set of skills to the challenges around us. We use our minds to become agents of meaningful change in our communities.

Not only is it possible to move in this direction; in my mind, it is imperative. What is your vision of the people of the future Commonwealth?

# 44

## WHERE DO YOU LIVE?

Every time I travel and meet new people, I'm at a loss when they ask, "Where do you live?" I can't quite figure out what to call this place, nor where we are. It seems to be a common problem. At the last general membership meeting of the Marianas Visitors' Authority, the *ad hoc* committee on branding acknowledged the difficulty in naming ourselves, and thus branding ourselves.

Officially, we're the Commonwealth of Northern Mariana Islands. That's a mouthful. And if you try to abbreviate it, "CNMI," that doesn't really mean anything to anyone who isn't from Micronesia.

I propose it's time for a name change. Name changes can be painful. I went through one myself. I grew up in a coal-mining town in the Appalachian mountains of Kentucky. There, before the era of "political correctness," no one wanted to make the effort to learn the name of some foreign kid. So, in the first grade the principal called the immigrant family into his office and told us that my name, the one my parents had given me when I was born, "just won't do in these parts – pick another." David is the name I picked. As

191

it turns out, in America, "David" is a much more marketable name than the one I was born with.

Our group of islands, what is commonly now known as the Commonwealth of Northern Mariana Islands, ought to be known either as the "Mariana Islands," or "Saipan." And we need to boldly state that we're located in the "South Pacific." Here is my reasoning.

For option A – Mariana Islands – it's part of our current official name. The word "Commonwealth" doesn't really add anything to our brand identity. It's a political designation, and a confusing one. Guam doesn't market itself as the "Territory of Guam," California doesn't call itself the "State of California," and members of other commonwealths, like the "Commonwealth of Virginia" don't include that in their designations. With branding, the shorter the better.

I also suggest that it's time to drop "Northern" from our name. Where are the "Southern" Mariana Islands? Is that Guam? Is that how we define ourselves – the place north of Guam?

I don't think that the word "north" has any role in the name of a tropical island. When people want to know where we are, I say, the "South Pacific." I am well aware that we are north of the equator, but the equator isn't the only frame of reference. Alabama is also north of the equator, but it's in the "South," even the "deep South." Most of our tourists and business partners hail from regions north of us. The North Pacific sounds like a cold, even inhospitable place – maybe somewhere up around Alaska or Vladivostok. Say "South Pacific" and people think palm trees, warm breezes, sandy shores and swaying hips. That's us! If I'm talking to a cartographer, I'll say "just north of the equator." The South Pacific is a concept, and we're conceptually in the South Pacific.

Now someone is sure to squawk that Guam is also part of the Mariana Islands, and tell us that we can't usurp the name for ourselves. Sure we can. Guam doesn't need the name. And there is precedence. A few years ago, what used to be known as "Western Samoa" changed its name to "Samoa," much to the chagrin of the people from American Samoa. The implication is that Western Samoa is the *real* Samoa. I think the same can be said for us in relation to the Mariana Islands. If someone asks, "Isn't Guam part of the Mariana Islands too?" we simply say, "They're Guam, we're the Marianas," or even "They're the southern Marianas." They'll live.

There is of course, also, option B – change the name of the island chain to "Saipan." Or the "Saipan Islands." Think of Hawaii. The archipelago is called Hawaii (or the Hawaiian Islands), and each island has its own name, including one of the islands which is known also as Hawaii (or more commonly as "The Big Island"). The same would work well here. There are two disadvantages to the "Saipan" designation. First, for some reason people think Saipan sounds Asian, maybe because it sounds a bit like Taipan or Taipei or Sampan. They think we're part of the continent of Asia. So "Saipan" may not be the best idea. Why change one confusing name into another confusing name? Also, it might be better for us to go by "Mariana Islands," and ruffle the feathers of just the folks in Guam, rather than go by "Saipan," and upset the people in Tinian and Rota and the Northern Islands.

I'm from the Mariana Islands. It's in the South Pacific. I live on the island of Saipan. I just wish it were official.

# 45

## THE GOLDEN RULE

We're dealing with all kinds of practical challenges here in the Marianas. We're not alone. There are social and economic challenges the world over. As valuable as it is to seek practical solutions to practical problems, I'm a firm believer that we must first identify guiding principles that will direct our problem-solving approach. Dive into the practical solutions without first identifying the underlying principles, and we're likely to drift away from our core values. This paragraph from *The Promise of World Peace* sums it up nicely:

> *"There are spiritual principles, or what some call human values, by which solutions can be found for every social problem. Any well-intentioned group can in a general sense devise practical solutions to its problems, but good intentions and practical knowledge are usually not enough. The essential merit of spiritual principle is that it not only presents a perspective which harmonizes with that which is immanent in human nature, it also induces an attitude, a dynamic, a will, an aspiration, which facilitate the discovery and implementation of practical measures. Leaders of*

*governments and all in authority would be well served in their efforts to solve problems if they would first seek to identify the principles involved and then be guided by them.*"[17]

One of the principles that I think we can agree upon is what is commonly known as "The Golden Rule." The version I learned in grade school stated, "Do unto others as you would have others do unto you." It makes sense and it resonates with most human beings. Unfortunately, it often gets lost when dealing with the social and economic problems we face.

The Golden Rule is universal and has woven its way through all the world's cultures and religions. Take a look.

Christianity – *"So in everything, do to others, what you would have them do to you, for this sums up the law and the prophets."*

Buddhism – *"Treat not others in ways that yourself would find hurtful."*

Bahá'í – *"Lay not on any soul a load that ye would not wish to be laid upon you, and desire not for anyone the things ye would not desire for yourself."*

Confucianism – *"One word which sums up the basis for all good conduct… loving-kindness. Do not do to others what you would not want done to yourself."*

Hinduism – *"This is the sum of duty: do not do to others what would cause pain if done to you."*

Islam – *"Not one of you truly believes until you wish for others what you wish for yourself."*

Judaism – *"What is hateful to you do not do to your neighbor."*

Zoroastrianism – *"Do not unto others what is injurious to yourself."*

At its core, the Golden Rule is an expression of the principle of the oneness of humanity – a recognition that the person across the table, across the street, across the island or across the water is just like you and wants to be treated just like you when it comes to basic issues. It seems simple, but its implications are vast, and it is these implications that seem to so often get lost in dealing with various issues.

Our community quickly spoke up that holding a sign that reads, "Go home!" is a violation of the principle of loving-kindness and of the Golden Rule. But what other practices stand against the Golden Rule and the principle of the oneness of humanity? How does legislation that takes into account one's birthplace or genetic composition jive with the Golden Rule? Should the color of one's skin or the color of one's passport affect one's access to opportunity and free enterprise? Is the Golden Rule violated when hiring and firing is done on the basis of family relations or party affiliation, rather than on the basis of merit?

When policy is based upon principles – universal spiritual values – the policies and positions will ring true. As we face larger challenges and more intricate issues, it would help us to think about the values upon which our practical solutions will be based. The Golden Rule is a good place to start. It will help us evaluate some of our basic assumptions about who we are and how we behave in relation to others, not just as individuals, but also as institutions.

# 46

## WORK ETHIC

On a recent Thursday evening, I was down at the Street Market and ran into a friend of mine, an attorney. As is common these days, talk quickly moved toward federalization and its associated issues, including the issue of work ethic. My friend pointed out that many people here are deprived of the opportunity to start working at the bottom of the ladder. Many do not want to take the "entry-level" job, seeing it as beneath them, mostly because of cultural expectations of which ethnicities perform which jobs. The two of us soon got to talking about our own experiences with entry-level jobs. He entered the work force as a cook. Many people in American society start out by waiting tables or pumping gas. It is here, in these entry-level positions, that a work ethic is born and nurtured. There is room for trial and error. There are lessons to be learned. When people skip to the front of the employment line, they miss out on some important experiences that help build their work ethic.

I started to think of my own early employment experiences. My first job was delivering newspapers. I was in elementary school, and our local newspaper employed a fleet of kids to deliver the newspapers door-to-door. Every morning the bundles of newspapers would get dropped off at my house. I would roll them up, put a rubber band around them, wrap them in plastic and set off on my bicycle with the newspaper sack hung over my shoulder, *Daily News* emblazoned on its side. I was proud of the job and did everything possible to keep the route. This job taught me that people relied on me and my services. If I didn't deliver the papers, they weren't happy. I learned to be reliable. My biggest fear was getting sick and not being able to deliver the papers, so I had a friend come with me on most days so that he would know the route. On the days I was sick, he would deliver the papers for me, and I'd pay him out of my small salary. Reliability, consistency, responsibility, customer service, planning, the need to show up even when I didn't feel like it – all of these I learned from a paper route.

My next job was cutting grass. When I was in junior high school, my buddy, George Givens, and I went door-to-door lining up customers, and we spent the summer mowing lawns. Hot sweaty work. Physical labor. We had about a dozen customers and we worked pretty much every day.

In high school, I worked in the school cafeteria washing dishes. There was no glory in that job, but I earned enough to pay some of my school expenses, and it was fun. We sang; we sprayed each other with water; we played the drums on the scrubbed pots. It was my first encounter with withholding taxes.

In college, hungry for exposure to the medical profession, I yearned to somehow get a job in an operating room. With no degree and no skill, the closest I could get was working in the recovery room of a hospital. I was assigned as an "orderly." As an orderly, you do whatever anyone orders you to do. (Or maybe you create order.) It's usually the work that no one else wants to do. I spent my hours taking inventory of medical supplies, stocking IV's on shelves, and emptying basins of vomit and jugs of pee produced by patients coming out of the stupor of anesthesia. I mopped the floors when I spilled the stuff. I gagged routinely.

All of these jobs helped me to form a work ethic: a sense of responsibility and a desire to excel at whatever I do. But more importantly, it left me with a connection to all the people in these and other forms of "menial labor." This value is being missed by those who, for whatever reason, won't take such jobs. There is dignity in honest work of any kind, and I'm grateful that these jobs were a part of my work history.

# 47

# SMILEY EELS AND BOONIE DOGS

Our family of six stopped by the drive-thru window of a local fast food restaurant because no one wanted to cook. Our older son, Arman, who is six, had recently taken a liking to the Smiley Meal. He didn't really like the food, but he really liked the toy, which is why, I suppose, it's there in the first place.

We pulled up to the little speaker. "Hello, welcome to Fast Food, may I take your order?" I'm guessing that's what she said. You know how those drive-thru speakers can be pretty crackly. "Yes, I'll have a blah, two blahs, one blah, and one Smiley Meal." "May I repeat your order, sir? That's one blah, two blahs, a blah, and one Smiley *Eel*."

Hmmm. I'm pretty sure I said "Smiley Meal" and she probably heard "Smiley Meal" and she may have even meant to say "Smiley Meal," and it may have just been the speaker crackling, but I'm sure she said "Smiley *Eel*." Here on the tropical island of Saipan, it would be quite possible to get a Smiley *Eel* at the local Fast Food place.

The scene flashes across my mind: Arman gets the Smiley Meal box. Everyone is opening their food. He sticks his hand into the box without looking and this smiling slithering sopping wet three-foot long eel latches onto his wrist with two-hundred tiny razor teeth. He screams! Everyone screams. Food flies! The eel won't let go! Arman is flailing his arm and the eel is swinging like a fat whip, smacking the other kids as they try to duck. Blood is spurting from Arman's wrist, splattering the inside of the windows. This is the scene that I imagine in that split second. Parents are programmed to imagine worst-case scenarios in an instant as part of an evolutionary mechanism to ensure the survival of the species while simultaneously keeping parents on the edge of insanity. I stare at the speaker and hear, "Sir, will that be all?"

I'm weighing my options. I mean, I really don't want to end up with a Smiley *Eel* instead of a Smiley Meal. I'd better clarify things, don't you think? Well, I break with long-standing character flaws and put my trust in the forces of the universe. "Yes, that will be all." "Thank you, next window please." I pull up with a sense of doom.

She passes the food though the window. The kids are eager. I (while still completely trusting in the forces of the universe, mind you), peek inside the Smiley Meal box. No eel. Whadya know. Silly me.

I pass everything back, shaking my head and chuckling at myself for my ridiculous imaginings. Arman gets his meal, thrusts his hand inside the box and pulls it out screaming! Food flies. Everyone is screaming. It's minivan pandemonium! "What in Ray Kroc is going on?" I wonder. "I checked the box. I swear I did!"

Tears are running down Arman's face as he clutches something in his small hand. "This isn't a toy!" he screams. "Look at this! This isn't a toy!" (Okay. This here is a little note for Arman's future college application reviewer or employer or fiancé or whoever decides to google Arman and comes across this column. I'm exaggerating, okay? Arman would never ever respond like this in real life. He's a great guy and emotionally solid. I'm using artistic license here. Plus, he's only six.)

I stare at the toy, as do all my other kids, and we agree with Arman's sentiments: What in the *h-e*-double-toothpicks is *that*? It's a sort of demented looking Sponge Bob pin-cushion thing-a-ma-bob. Not much you can do with it, except look at it (which isn't easy) and throw it away.

Which brings me to my point (yes, there is one). What are they thinking up there at worldwide Fast Food corporate headquarters? These toys last thirty seconds, fill the dump with unnecessary mass, end up in the ocean, or worse, my sock drawer, and have little redeeming value beyond the sale. A toy like this just isn't very satisfying.

Here is what I propose (and I speak on behalf of all parents). Instead of adding these cheap little toys to the meal, throw in something that will last. Something that will bring joy. Something that will love you back. Throw in a puppy. A cute, warm, fuzzy, adorable puppy. (Or even, say, a live chicken.) Now that would be something to cheer about; something to live with and grow with; a pet! And here on Saipan, it would help address both the solid-waste problem (by eliminating the toy) and the stray dog (and chicken) issue. Run a joint promotion with PAWS. Include a Boonie Dog with every Fast Food meal. "Would you like a mangy Wiener dog with your Big Deal Fish Meal, Ma'am?" Now we're talkin'! "Sir, can we Double-Size that to a Boonie-with-a-Tumor for you?" Yeah, buddy!

Sure, it'll take a little extra training to figure out how to safely pass the critters through the take-out window, across the gap, and into the car window (probably tail first), but it'll be worth it. We face a multiplicity of serious issues on our islands, and this is one solution that can definitively address several of our mounting problems simultaneously. The landfill wins, the stray dogs (and chickens) win, the children win, the whole island wins! This is a real solution to a real problem. Let's generate some discussion on this. Do you think a Boonie Dog offer with every Fast Food Meal with help eradicate the stray dog problem, while simultaneously decreasing solid waste?

# 48

## THE TIDE

When we are young, nature moves us forward. Our bodies grow and develop effortlessly. Without trying, our bones and muscles grow stronger, our vitality increases, our cardio-vascular capacity propels forward. We are riding on a rising tide.

Then, the tide changes. It actually happens fairly early in life. In our twenties, the effortless growth stops, and a slow decay starts. This shift takes a while to notice, and most of us who are relatively healthy may not feel any change in our vitality until we reach our late thirties or early forties. But the tide has been moving us back for a decade. We don't know it until we wake up one morning feeling creaky.

A year ago, I noticed the tide had pulled me out. I had horrible pain in my lower back, and spent a few days of the summer lying flat on my back. I saw a doctor, and was diagnosed with just lower back pain – nothing serious, except that it was debilitating. It seemed like everything I tried to do was met with some new pain. I resolved to exercise, and started doing push-ups, only to get an ache in my wrist. I tried to run, and was so out of breath that I just gave up.

I, like many people, believed that from this point forward, I had started my slow gradual decline to the grave — each year, a little weaker, a little sicker, a little more creaky, until finally, we reach the bottom and get buried.

If this is your image of your life (or if this is what you're experiencing) it doesn't have to be that way. You don't have to let the tide carry you out. The truth is, you can fight the tide, and stay healthy and active your entire life, until say, the final year. This is one of the most important truths to recognize: you can fight the tide. Instead of slowly declining until you reach the bottom, you can ride flat across the plateau, healthy and strong until almost the end of the ride, and then crumble in your nineties. You don't have to go through a gradual decline that starts in your forties. You can stay strong and active and then decline just before you die.

There are three things you need to do to fight the tide. I'll talk about one of them today. It's the one I hate. It's called exercise. To fight the tide, you need to exercise six days a week. Four of those days need to be rigorous aerobic exercise. I mean exercise that makes you sweat and breath hard. For thirty minutes. The exercise on two of the days can be resistance training, like weight-lifting. Exercise is the single most important step toward keeping you strong and active and fighting the tide. It is a fundamental truth, and I hate the truth, but it's still the truth: six days a week of exercise to fight the tide and stay healthy into your eighties and nineties. Remember, the tide is there every day. Any day that you don't exercise, is a day that you're letting the tide pull you out.

After facing this reality, I decided to suck it up and start doing what I needed to do to live the way I want to live for the next forty or fifty years. I don't want to get weaker every year. I don't want to spend the last decade of my life tied to a chair. I want to play hard and be fit and just collapse and crumble in my last year of life. Fighting the tide can actually make your body younger. Since starting my exercise regimen, my back pain has vanished, I'm stronger, I can run two miles (which isn't much, but it's much farther than before), and I have more vitality and energy. That's definitely a younger body than I was living with last year.

As most of us move into our forties and beyond, this tide becomes the dominant force defining our health. Fighting it can ensure that the next fifty years are active and healthy until the end. It's never too late to start. If you are in your sixties or seventies, you can still have a younger body next year, and make some significant gains on the tide. No matter your age, it's possible. Just check with your doctor before starting any exercise regimen. And if you want to learn more, pick up a copy of the book, *Younger Next Year*, by Chris Crowley and Henry S. Lodge, MD.

# 49

## SEX, CANCER VACCINES AND RESTRAINT

A new vaccine is now available to the CNMI's school age girls to vaccinate against cervical cancer. Cervical cancer is a devastating disease which strikes 10,000 women a year in the US (with 4,000 deaths per year) and an estimated 500,000 women around the world. It is particularly tragic because it often strikes mothers while their families are young. Seventy percent of cervical cancer is caused by strains of the human papillomavirus (HPV). The vaccine prevents infection by the virus, thereby preventing up to 7,000 cases of cervical cancer in the US per year. Cervical cancer can occur for other reasons. In fact, smoking doubles your risk of cervical cancer. So the vaccine is not a cure-all. But it will make a significant dent in the incidence of the disease and it will hopefully be another triumph of medicine over disease.

I was having a discussion recently with a friend of mine who is a health official here in the CNMI about this vaccine, and our conversation soon turned to some of the unexamined issues surrounding cervical cancer. Yes, most cervical cancer is caused by a virus, and preventing infection by the virus with the vaccine is a good thing. But how do you get the virus? Do you get it from a cough or a sneeze or from shaking hands? No. You get the infection through sexual intercourse. It is a sexually transmitted virus, and ultimately, a sexually transmitted cancer. Early onset of sexual activity and multiple sexual partners increases the risk of infection and ultimately, of cancer. That's why we're giving the vaccine to girls who are eleven and twelve years old (it's approved for girls as young as nine). Our unexamined assumption is that these young girls will lead promiscuous lives, thereby putting themselves at risk for encountering the virus.

As my friend and I were talking, he wondered out loud if we were enabling promiscuous sexual behavior with the vaccine. It's a thorny question, like wondering if handing out condoms to prevent HIV leads to promiscuity. He also wondered about the silence on our island regarding sexuality and promiscuity, and if our tightly knit families are also in some way supporting promiscuous behaviors. There are very few messages out there, particularly from mothers and fathers, telling our children to restrain their sexuality. The relative silence is deafening. Families are loving and accepting of teenage pregnancy and by extension, of teenage sex. Babies are born to unmarried high-school girls. The grandma and aunties help the mother, and raise the child with warmth and love and care. It's a good thing, I think, and it doesn't need to be viewed simply as "enabling behavior," but it does need balance. There needs to be some loud and constant voice that guides a child toward appropriate expression of sexuality.

From what I understand, there was a time, not too long ago, when here in the Marianas, in our local culture, there was a real stigma attached to premarital sex and pregnancy. Things have changed. My friend tells me that families no longer promote sexual restraint, and our social and religious institutions likewise, have fallen silent on the issue.

I'm not a "fire-and-brimstone-you're-going-to-burn-in-hell-for-sinning" sort of guy. But I do believe that sexual restraint is a good thing and that it ought to be openly taught to our children (despite what we ourselves may have done). I'm not a "sex-is-the-root-of-evil" sort of guy either, and I believe that sex and sexuality are gifts to humanity. It is a wonderful human impulse which should not be suppressed, but which should be regulated and controlled. I believe sex is a spiritual act and that its highest and most meaningful expression takes place within marriage. I also believe people should marry young, if they're ready (whatever that means), and thus fully enjoy their sexuality in their prime.

These ideas run counter to the *Fotten Gaga* culture that has emerged – the wild animal with no restraint. Keep saying nothing, and this lack of restraint, in all areas, will overrun us. The ability to restrain oneself, whether sexually or otherwise, is a great skill – one to be taught, encouraged and promoted. We each have all sorts of impulses. It's not the impulses that are the problem, but the inability to control them (or the fact that no one ever told us that we ought to control them). It seems that most of the violations of law and ethics that we see in our community arise simply from people's lack of self-restraint – lack of effort to regulate and control their impulses.

Now, I'm not saying that all social ills, all crime and corruption, emerge because kids are boinking between the stacks of the school library. I am saying that we could use a louder voice guiding them away from sexual promiscuity, toward self-restraint. I'm saying that if we're going to swab our daughters arms with alcohol and push a needle through their skin, we ought to at least be telling them to keep their pants on – that the vaccine is "just in case," not "so that you can." Our sons need to hear it too.

# 50

## MAGIC AND MEDICINE

Sometimes a patient comes in and wants to test the competence of the doctor before trusting the doctor with her care. That happened to me today.

Mrs. Marcos, as I'll call her, is in her sixties. Like many people on Saipan who are part of non-Western cultures, her world-view has not been significantly influenced by the laws of physics. Ordinary objects and people appear, disappear, morph, transmute, and each with some intent, either to effect good or evil. The world is magical, like the world in Gabriel Garcia Marquez' *One Hundred Years of Solitude*. If you're going to successfully practice medicine here, you have to embrace this world-view. You have to recognize that your Western scientific world-view is just that: one particular world-view. If you want to gain people's trust and help them change, you have to do it from within their world-view, not by getting them to accept your world-view. That would be an affront to their view. It would be regarded as disrespectful.

Mrs. Marcos told me that there was nothing wrong with her eyes. She was just here for a routine eye exam. "Okay, let me see if there are any problems." After a few seconds of looking at her eye under magnification, I say, "Mrs. Marcos, you have a cyst full of fluid on your eye. Have you noticed it?" She looks stunned. I've uncovered a secret. I've seen it. I must be trustworthy.

She becomes animated. "Doc, let me tell you the story of how this happened." Now, I'll admit, when a patient in my exam room offers to tell me a story, I get a little nervous. Stories take time, and there are lots of people outside my door waiting to see me. But I learned long ago to be attentive to the person in front of me. She continues. "I was asleep in my room one night. It was two months ago. A man came in and I awoke. He seemed like an ordinary man, but he was this tall." She holds her hand at shin height, indicating that he was a miniature man. "He came into my room. I heard the sound. I saw him but I was scared, so I pretended not to. The next night he came back with a woman who also seemed ordinary, but was like him. They keep coming back to bother me night after night, making noise. One night they climbed into the ceiling. They stayed there and every night they throw pepper into my eyes and wake me up. They are the ones that caused this bump on my eye!" She's agitated. She's crying, tortured by the burning in her eyes, and the evil little people that are causing her pain. I take her hand and listen. "It sounds very frightening," I say. "Would you like me to take that bump off?" "Please, yes."

She's not crazy. In her world, there are explanations for illnesses that are not based upon the germ theory of disease or Starling's law or biochemistry. Try to talk her out of her world-view, and you'll lose all credibility. You'll cut your own legs out from under yourself. You'll eliminate yourself as a doctor she can trust to help her. But you can't just tolerate her world-view. You have to approach her with humility, recognizing that your world-view makes sense to you, but it's not the only one, maybe not even the right one; just one that works for you.

We set up the tiny little scissors and forceps and in about thirty seconds the mass is removed from her eye. She is completely relieved and she is comforted by my words that if it comes back, I'm here with my own little bit of magic.

# 51

# GROSS NATIONAL HAPPINESS

There is an unexamined assumption that is controlling our lives, and it is this: the more we have, the happier we'll be. We may say, "money can't buy happiness," but we sure don't act like we believe it. Every effort seems to be focused on economic improvement, as if that will automatically lead to happiness. The unspoken assumption is that the more money we have, and the more goods we consume, the happier we will be. Though we don't articulate it, we're really not seeking economic growth. We're seeking happiness. But financial well-being and happiness have come to be so strongly connected that we never really think to separate them. We don't even ask, "Are they really the same thing?"

When I think back over my own experiences, the happiest days of my adult life were the ones I was the poorest. Is the richest man in the world also the happiest man in the world? Sure, greater economic resources do provide certain benefits, but those benefits do not have a direct correlation to happiness.

Which would you rather have right now: more money or more happiness? This is a tough question because the false connection between money and happiness is so strong that for many of us, there is a reluctance to choose "more happiness." We don't believe that we could actually be more happy without more money. We are also tempted to choose "more money," because deep down we believe that by having more money we will automatically get happiness. But, really, shouldn't we all be choosing, without any hesitation, "more happiness"?

In 1972 when the new king of the Himalayan nation of Bhutan was crowned, he declared that he was more concerned with "Gross National Happiness" (GNH) than "Gross National Product" (GNP). He felt that it was a more accurate reflection of the well-being of a society to look directly at its happiness, rather than presuming that consumption (GNP) reflected the nation's well-being.

As our own economy seems to spiral downward, ideas emerge to improve the economy. The worse the economy gets, the more desperate the ideas become; their proponents seem to believe that with more money, everything will be okay and we'll be happier.

I like the idea of Gross National Happiness, and I think that it's time we pay a little more attention to it here in the Marianas. We may not be too familiar with it, but GNH has been called the most significant advancement in economic theory in the past 150 years, simply because it seeks to measure actual well-being rather than consumption.

According to Wikipedia, *"the concept of GNH claims to be based on the premise that true development of human society takes place when material and spiritual development occur side by side to complement and reinforce each other."* GNH has four pillars: the promotion of equitable and sustainable socio-economic development; preservation and promotion of cultural values; conservation of the natural environment; and establishment of good governance. Sounds pretty good, don't you think?

Happiness is serious stuff, and over the past thirty years, the idea of GNH has gradually taken hold in countries around the world. Government officials, economists, foundations, policy centers and NGO's from around the world gather regularly for GNH conferences.

Happiness is an area that doesn't get the attention it deserves. We confuse it with economic development, which although an element of happiness, is not the complete picture. As we begin to give focused attention to happiness, our perspective and direction will shift to more holistic approaches that take into account the spiritual dimensions of our island society. It's not far out to envision that as we come to understand its importance, we will one day have a cabinet level Secretary of Happiness or a Special Assistant for Happiness. We already have these positions; we just call them something else because we don't recognize that fundamentally, it's happiness we're seeking. Let's focus on Gross National Happiness. It's a real concept with real indicators to be measured, followed, and addressed.

# 52

## GECKO TAILS

I was rather amazed by the speed and agility of my two-year-old son. The other day he caught a gecko. He held it gently as he showed it to me. But my proud smile turned to horror as he nonchalantly ripped its tail off. If you know anything about geckos you know that if its tail gets pulled off, the detached tail stays alive for a while, and the gecko goes off to grow a new one. But still, no one wants their kid to start torturing animals at such a young age.

As I watched the gecko's tail having its seizure on the floor, an image poked out of the crevices of my brain: a tongue in a metal basin. It was my first week on the oncology ward during my training. Our team of twelve – a professor, two residents, some interns, a few medical students and an oncology nurse – was making our morning rounds, stopping by each patient's room, and making a plan for their treatment for the day. We went to the bedside of a man, asked how he was doing, and before any of us knew what was happening, the professor grasped the man's tongue with a piece of gauze, cut the thing off, and handed it to the oncology nurse. She plunked the cancer-ridden tongue into a metal basin. I stood there aghast at what had so suddenly and impetuously transpired. I looked at the tongue in the metal basin, as it silently moved for a few seconds, desperately trying to speak. The twitching gecko tail had released this image from its locked cage in my dim memory, and it rushed forth like a demon let loose from the depths of hell. Just thought you'd like to know. Sweet dreams.

As I thought about this later (the tail, not the tongue), I realized that the gecko's tail is in many ways a metaphor for various aspects of island life. First of all, it is a symbol of fecundity. You just can't prevent things from growing on a tropical island. You can't beat back the boonies for long; you can't keep the black mold off the painted walls; you can't keep the ants away from the kitchen counter; you have to shave twice a day. Everything grows and reproduces – rapidly. I've cut down banana trees and returned to their stumps just hours later to find a new tree growing. I've gotten innocent scrapes that in a day oozed with bacteria-laden pus. I've gone away for a long weekend, returned late and tired, thrown back the sheets, only to find that two inches of fuzzy mold had grown between the covers. That's life in the tropics: plenty heat; plenty water; the gecko's tail grows back.

Then there's the gecko's detached tail – the part that gets cut off and keeps on living, wriggling, undulating. In a close, small, isolated island community, stories, news, rumors and speculations easily detach from their sources and live within the community for no apparent reason. Wonder out loud if a typhoon is coming, and within hours, twenty thousand people will be saying they "heard" a typhoon is coming. Talk of anything – politics, labor, immigration, federalization, you name it – can end up living independently, far removed from its source. Ideas detach and gain a life of their own. Even if an idea or story or speculation dies, it doesn't take much effort to grow the tail back.

For the gecko, its detached tail does serve a purpose. As my son became mesmerized by the wiggling piece of tail that lay on the floor calling out to him, "Look at me! Look over here!" his attention drifted from the rest of the gecko, alive but silent and still, in the palm of his other hand. His inattentive grip loosened, and the gecko scampered away. Get in trouble, and all you have to do is call attention to some writhing distraction, while the real issue is forgotten and you run away. This ploy works all the time, and not just on an island. It seems to be a universal phenomenon. But here, once you see a gecko without a tail, you gain a deeper appreciation of how important the distraction can be to a creature's very survival.

Now, if I could only stop thinking about that tongue...

# EPILOGUE

Thank you for taking the time to read this book. I believe that the world is what we make of it. Our experience of it has more to do with who we are than with what the world presents to us. Novel ideas, fresh perspectives and new information can all lead to insights. New insights change who we are, and thus change our experience of the world. It is my hope that these pieces have helped make your life a little happier and healthier. I hope the bits of laughter along the way have helped make the journey a little lighter.

Tell me what you liked, the insights you may have gained, the changes that came about, or how you see the world differently. We writers so rarely receive feedback. Feel free to contact me through my publisher, Tiningo Press, or send me an email – davidkhorram@gmail.com. I look forward to hearing from you.

# Notes

[1] Bahá'í International Community, *The Prosperity of Humankind*. Wilmette: Bahá'í Publishing Trust, 1995.

[2] 'Abdu'l-Bahá', in Lady Blomfield, *The Chosen Highway*. Wilmette, IL: Bahá'í Publishing Trust, 1954, p. 167.

[3] 'Abdu'l-Bahá', in *The Compilation of Compilations*, prepared by the Universal House of Justice 1963 – 1990. Mona Vale, NSW: Bahá'í Publications Australia, 1991. pp. 11-14

[4] Bahá'u'lláh, *Gleanings from the Writings of Bahá'u'lláh*. Wilmette, IL: Bahá'í Publishing Trust, 1938. p. 286

[5] ibid

[6] From a letter written on behalf of Shoghi Effendi, May 12, 1925, in *Lights of Guidance*, compiled by Helen Hornby. New Dehli: Bahá'í Publishing Trust, 2nd ed. 1988. p. 92

[7] 'Abdu'l-Bahá', quoted in a letter written on behalf of the Universal House of Justice, August 13, 1980, in *Lights of Guidance*, compiled by Helen Hornby. New Dehli: Bahá'í Publishing Trust, 2nd ed. 1988. p. 89

[8] Kurzius, Brian, *Fire and Gold – Benefiting from Life's Tests*. Oxford: George Ronald, 1995. p. xi

[9] 'Abdu'l-Bahá', *Paris Talks*. London: Bahá'í Publishing Trust, 1967. p. 50

[10] ibid. p. 178

[11] 'Abdu'l-Bahá', in Shoghi Effendi, *The Advent of Divine Justice*. Wilmette, IL: Bahá'í Publishing Trust, 1966. p. 22

[12] Bernice Johnson Reagon, *I Remember I Believe* on the CD *Sacred Ground* by Sweet Honey in the Rock. EarthBeat Records, 1995. Track 1

[13] Shoghi Effendi, in The Universal House of Justice, *The Promise of World Peace*, Wilmette, IL: Bahá'í Publishing Trust, 1985. sec. I, para. 13

[14] The Universal House of Justice, Letter to the World's Religious Leaders, April 2002. para. 25

[15] Bahá'u'lláh, *Gleanings from the Writings of Bahá'u'lláh*. Wilmette, IL: Bahá'í Publishing Trust, 1938. p. 298

[16] Letter from the Universal House of Justice, dated January 4, 1994, in National Spiritual Assembly of the Bahá'ís of the United States, *Developing Distinctive Bahá'í Communities*. Wilmette, IL: Bahá'í Publishing Trust. p. 10.47

[17] The Universal House of Justice, *The Promise of World Peace*, Wilmette, IL: Bahá'í Publishing Trust, 1985. sec. II, para. 13